# WHAT PEOPLE ARE SAYING ABOUT THIS BOOK

'This important, timely book gives the reader an invaluable insight into the workings of the world of social entrepreneurship. It is a must-read for students, practitioners, policy makers and anyone with a passing interest in how to work for the greater good.'
**Professor Klaus Schwab**, Founder of the World Economic Forum and Co-Founder of the Schwab Foundation for Social Entrepreneurship

'This book's vivid, engaging stories – of ordinary people who have devoted their lives to solving problems and injustices they never expected to encounter – make a major contribution to understanding what social innovation is all about. This is an inspiring and essential read for everyone who cares about our flawed, messy, beautiful world and believes in its myriad possibilities.'
**Hannah Bloch**, Mission Projects Editor, *National Geographic* magazine

'Ken Banks, whose own career has taken him from offshore banking to launching a brilliant communications tool for Africa, takes us on a social innovation journey. We meet ten entrepreneurs who happened on life-changing ideas – from solar lighting for African maternity wards to film subtitles to promote literacy in India – and then fought against every kind of obstacle to make them happen. Inspiring and instructive.'
**Rory Cellan-Jones**, BBC Technology Correspondent

'Ken Banks offers us inspiration, wisdom and reluctance in just the right measure to help make lasting social innovation a discipline that others can help create and sustain, rather than having it remain an unfulfilled pipe dream.'
**Cheryl Heller**, Founding Chair, MFA Design for Social Innovation at the School of Visual Arts, New York

'Ken's work has transformed the lives of many people and shown how the appropriate application of technology can change the world for the better. In this important book he has generously brought together tales from other "reluctant entrepreneurs" to show how inspiration and application can begin to address the world's pressing problems. It's a great read, and a vital message.'
**Bill Thompson**, Writer, broadcaster, commentator for *Click* (on BBC World Service radio) and Visiting Professor at the Royal College of Art

'There's a lot of hyperbole at the intersection of technology and social entrepreneurship, but you won't find any in here. This important book describes how pressing social problems are being creatively solved with appropriate technology by gifted people. Inspirational stuff!'
**Alex van Someren**, Managing Partner of Early Stage Funds,
Amadeus Capital Partners

'If these ten extraordinary people are defined as reluctant then the world needs more of these Tesla-esque entrepreneurs, thinkers and doers who have engineered similarly game-changing innovations whose impact will be as profound as the enigmatic Nikola. Bravo to their brilliance.'
**Toby Shapshak**, Editor, *Stuff* magazine

'Many of us are looking for ways to combine our passion and purpose in life and this book provides some great tips. This book is filled with stories that inspire us to remember the road is not always easy and tenacity and time are critical parts of the journey. The great news is that it really is possible to change the world – one marvellous reluctant innovator at a time!'
**Grace Killelea**, Founder and CEO of Half the Sky Leadership Institute
and 2011 Multichannel News Wonder Woman

'This book is a refreshing antidote to pessimism about the potential of individuals influencing "social change". The author of each chapter has a personal story to tell, but each in such a way that it helps us to better understand the different ways it is possible to make that change happen.'
**Dr Elizabeth Harrison**, Reader in Anthropology and former Head of
International Development, University of Sussex

'What an inspiration! This book is a testament that we can all make a much bigger difference in the world than we ever dreamed possible. It has encouraged me to take bigger and bolder steps in my own foundation, "Together we can Change the World", and in my business as well. Read it and treat yourself to a new way of thinking.'
**Scott Friedman**, Chief Celebration Officer at Scott Friedman & Associates and
author of *Celebrate! Lessons Learned from the World's Most Admired Organizations*

'*The Rise of the Reluctant Innovator* tells the poignant stories of entrepreneurs with such perseverance and passion that will be an inspiration to all those hoping to make a difference in the world. And it is an important reminder of the sacrifice that community leaders and development professionals make as they tackle the most pressing problems plaguing the world today.'
**Priya Jaisinghani**, Deputy Director of Innovation and
Development Alliances, USAID

'*The Rise of the Reluctant Innovator* gives an incredibly rare, personal and enlightening account of social entrepreneurs around the world. Their innovations demonstrate how technology can be a potent force for positive change in the world.'
**Katie Jacobs Stanton**, Vice President of International Market Development, Twitter

'A revelatory view of world-changing innovators. Read these pages to find that life-passions are revealed in the most unconventional manner, and discover the path to success consists of battling enormous obstacles.'
**John Siceloff**, Emmy Award Winner and Founder/CEO of CatchTheNext.org

'These real – occasionally raw – stories do more to capture the life of the committed social entrepreneur than anything else I've read. Inspiring, yes, but even better, it works as a real world case-based manual for how to create change for the better.'
**Kevin Starr**, Managing Director, Mulago Foundation

'It seems that around the world we are witnessing a new collective consciousness of sorts. There is a heightened awareness of the need to help others. We feel compelled to have a real impact on the "bigger picture" and to do more for the "greater good". Social entrepreneurship is on the rise, and this book shines much needed light on how to transform inspiration into innovation.'
**Darice Fisher**, Public Relations and Media Expert

'Ken Banks is the quintessential explorer, driven by curiosity and purpose, strengthened by obstacles, and culturally mindful. In *The Rise of the Reluctant Innovator*, Ken – a collaborator by nature – has swung the spotlight onto the heroic work of a group of driven individuals who are creating a better future for people and communities around the world. Transcending trendy terms and structured models around social entrepreneurship, Ken's common theme is one of possibility and empowerment – anyone can effect social change. I believe this collection of stories of passion and impact will leave people hungering for more and will inspire more than a few readers to explore their passions and translate them into incremental stories of meaningful change.'
**Alex Moen**, Vice President of Explorer Programs, National Geographic

'*The Rise of the Reluctant Innovator* is required reading for any student or anyone interested in technology-based invention to improve peoples' lives, and social innovation as a potential life path. Its honest stories of unforeseen challenges and unexpected opportunities from the people encountering them both are an inspiration and refreshing reality-check.'
**Joshua Schuler**, Executive Director, Lemelson–MIT Program

'Ken Banks has assembled compelling, insightful first-person accounts from re-markable people pursuing social change through technology. The book will be inspiring and informative to many others on similar paths.'
**Jonathan Donner**, Technology for Emerging Markets Group, Microsoft Research

'Read this book and be inspired. And ask the question it poses: Can I, in however lesser-a-way, also find my passion, become a social entrepreneur and make our world a better place?'
**Robert Chambers**, Research Associate, Institute of Development Studies at the University of Sussex

'As a pioneer in this field Ken knows more than anyone what it is to be a reluctant innovator. This is an inspiring book introducing us to those who have changed their worlds with their simple, elegant ideas.'
**Chris Locke**, Managing Director, GSMA Mobile for Development

'As a social entrepreneur, educator and facilitator I believe these times call for innovation from all points in the spectrum, especially those of us that are un-reasonable enough to hope we can make change in the world. Thank you for this book – it is just what the field needs!'
**Rebecca Saltman**, Disruptive Innovator and Educator,
A Foot in the Door Productions

'A fascinating and insightful work. This book will serve as a guide and source of inspiration for all who seek to change the world.'
**Terry Garcia**, Executive Vice President of Mission Programs,
National Geographic

'Why would anyone trade a life of comfort for the muddy boots of change-mak-ing? Ken Banks shows how global challenges trouble the waters of our con-science, and compel a new generation of innovators to action.'
**Andrew Zolli**, Executive Director and Curator, PopTech

'The world's most challenging problems are being taken on by people motivated by their personal passions, informed by their deep understanding of local real-ities and shaped by their frustration with inadequate solutions. Ken Banks and the other remarkable innovators here offer inspiration and insight into building practical solutions while calling into question established wisdom about social innovation. This is a must-read book for anyone who wants to solve problems with global implications through local knowledge and involvement.'
**Ethan Zuckerman**, Director of the Center for Civic Media, MIT

The Rise of the Reluctant Innovator

# THE RISE OF THE
# RELUCTANT INNOVATOR

Edited by
## Ken Banks

LONDON PUBLISHING PARTNERSHIP

Published by London Publishing Partnership
www.londonpublishingpartnership.co.uk

ISBN: 978-1-907994-18-0 (pbk.)

A catalogue record for this book is
available from the British Library

This book has been composed in Cambria
by T&T Productions Ltd, London

Copy-editing by Tim Knight

Cover image: Laura Stachel, We Care Solar

Printed in the United Kingdom by
Hobbs the Printers Ltd

*In memory of a wonderful
and supportive mother,
and for Henry, Madeleine
and Oliver, whom she
sadly never got to meet*

# Table of Contents

# TABLE OF CONTENTS

# ACKNOWLEDGEMENTS

It would be almost impossible to recognise everyone who has helped, encouraged and supported me and my work over the years, so this list is by no means exhaustive.

A few of these people include the late Freddie Cooper, who let me loose on his Commodore PET computer as a teenager, giving rise to what turned into a life-long career in IT. To Kevin Daly, Vanessa Nash and the late Ray Middleton who helped open my eyes to Africa, and Karen Hayes and Simon Hicks for calling me from my hospital bed and giving me a career-changing opportunity in mobile. To Sussex University for seeing my potential and letting me study there, Erik Sundelof who encouraged me later to apply to Stanford University (where my work finally took off) and to Stuart Gannes for accepting my Fellowship application the second time around.

To Jerry Huang and John Bracken at the MacArthur Foundation for taking a leap of faith and being the first to fund me, and to the coalition of Nigerian NGOs whose use of FrontlineSMS in their 2007 elections turned into the breakthrough story I so badly needed. To Bill Thompson, Jon Fildes and Gareth Mitchell at the BBC for breaking that story, and Larry Diamond for his unwavering support and friendship throughout. To the driver of the car in Calabar whose poor driving ended up changing the course of my life for the better, and to everyone else who helped me heal. To Daniel Epstein at the Unreasonable Institute who made me an offer to mentor social entrepreneurs on a ship that was too crazy to refuse, and Tori Hogan for inviting me to share her stage on board with Archbishop Desmond Tutu. And to Archbishop

Tutu for his friendship, mentorship, faith, unwavering optimism, and support for this book.

A special thanks also goes to Cliff Curry and Delight Stone from the Curry Stone Foundation, who have shown incredible friendship and support not just with this book, but for my wider work and ambitions.

Finally, to my family, who have never quite understood what it is I do for a living but have supported me nonetheless.

The very warmest of thanks and appreciation to each of them, and everyone else whose paths have crossed with mine over many years.

*Ken Banks*
*St Ives, Cambridgeshire, UK*

# FOREWORD

## Archbishop Desmond Tutu

For the world to be a better place for everyone, each of us needs to stand up against wrongs, show compassion and humility to others, and not turn our backs when we encounter hardship and suffering. These simple rules have guided me throughout my life, as they do for countless others who fight for the rights of the poor, marginalised and disenfranchised around the world.

That world is a much smaller place than it used to be. Thanks to the spread of the Internet and social media, many of these people's stories are being heard for the first time. Add to that the increasing numbers of young people wanting to make a difference in their lives, and we have all the makings of a positive force for change. It is my belief that it is down to each of us to help galvanise that change, and through his efforts with this book, Ken Banks clearly feels the same.

I had the pleasure of working with Ken during a recent voyage with Semester at Sea. Semester at Sea helps students get a better under-standing of our world by giving them the opportunity to spend one university term out of the classroom travelling the globe aboard a ship, the *MV Explorer*. Ken was on a five-week leg of the same journey, mentoring technology-focused social entrepreneurs with Unreasonable at Sea. Towards the end of his time I had the opportunity to sit with him, and author Tori Hogan, in front of an auditorium full of students to talk frankly about how they can make a difference in the world. Everyone there was hungry for knowledge and opportunity, which I very much hope we gave them. Today's youth are not only the problem solvers but also the leaders of the future.

It is in that spirit of shared learning that I have pleasure in introducing this exciting new book. *The Rise of the Reluctant Innovator* is a collection of real-life stories that show what's possible if people are open, take an interest and don't take the easy option of turning their back, but instead doggedly search for answers to problems effecting not just the people in front of them but, in many cases, tens of millions of other people around the world.

Read this book and you quickly realise that these stories have changed the lives of the innovators themselves as much as the people they set out to help. It is a book of hope, inspiration, and a beacon of what's possible.

*Archbishop Desmond Tutu*
*Cape Town, South Africa*

The Rise of the Reluctant Innovator

# INTRODUCTION

## Ken Banks

*'Don't ask yourself what the world needs. Ask yourself what makes you come alive and then go do that. Because what the world needs is people who come alive.'*

*Howard Thurman (1899–1981)*

## AN IDEA IS BORN (AGAIN)

This book has the unlikeliest of origins. It all started at 37,000 feet with a chance meeting with David Rowan, editor of *Wired* magazine's UK edition, in the aisle of a chartered flight to Johannesburg. It was June 2011. Dozens of journalists milled around, plotting in the back of the plane, with Prime Minister David Cameron and his ministerial colleagues camped up front. We sat in the middle, part of a fifty-strong

1

British government business delegation set to visit South Africa, Nigeria, Rwanda and South Sudan over four days. We spent more time in the air than we did on the ground, and didn't even make it to our last two destinations. It turns out that four days, however well planned, is a long time in politics.

A few months after our return, David recounted our high-altitude conversations and decided to get back in touch. He wanted me to write an article for their 'Ideas Bank', something that 'people would want to talk about down the pub'. This somewhat limited my options. I dug deep into my drawer of half-thought-out ideas and dusted one down from several years earlier which sketched out what I'd begun calling 'reluctant innovation'. Things that people had either fixed or discovered by accident, or reluctantly, struck a chord with the 'Ideas Bank' theme and 'Genius Happens When You Plan Something Else' appeared in the May 2012 edition of the magazine.

The original article was short, so I was only able to briefly highlight the stories of two innovators. But the seed of an idea was reborn, and the concept of 'reluctant innovation' grabbed my imagination once more. I felt there was a much bigger story to tell, and many more reluctant innovators to seek out. Numerous calls for contributors, hundreds of emails, masses of editing and reading, cover and chapter design sessions, failed funding campaigns and eighteen months later, 600 words became 70,000 and the book you are holding in your hands today was born.

The half-baked idea that somehow turned into this book began to emerge several years earlier during my time at Stanford University – a whole story in itself – where I became increasingly exposed to social entrepreneurship, social innovation and design thinking as academic disciplines. I found myself meeting increasing numbers of smart young people looking to colleges and universities to equip them with the skills they felt they needed to 'go out and change the world'. I was a bit taken aback. You didn't need qualifications to change the world, did you? Often I'd dig deeper and ask what they wanted to do when they graduated. Answers such as 'I want to be a social entrepreneur' perplexed me. Few people I know in the messy, often frustrating world of social entrepreneurship ever set out with the explicit aim of becoming one. Rather, they stumbled across a problem, a wrong or a market inefficiency which bothered them to such an extent that they decided to dedicate much – if not all – of their lives to putting it right. It was rarely, if ever, part of a wider plan.

Many of the students I met were unlikely to experience that problem, wrong, injustice or market inefficiency within the walls of their college or university. Teaching the mechanics of social innovation may be helpful, yes, but only if matched with passion, and a cause, to which people can apply it. Desperately seeking that one thing that switches you on can be a lonely, difficult journey. I speak from personal experience. But more of that later.

What I was witnessing was the increasing institutionalisation of social entrepreneurship. I thought it unhelpful on many fronts, not to mention that it could easily be seen as a barrier by many motivated young people. Not only that, it implied that social change was a well-thought out process, when in reality it is far messier and random than that, as many of the stories here testify. It's an important message that I hope this book manages to get across.

Of course, it is far easier to learn the mechanics of social entrepreneurship – business plans and elevator pitches among them – than to manufacture a passion or a calling in life. You may be the person best-qualified to solve a particular problem in the world, but that's of little use if you don't find it. Finding purpose is often the toughest part of the process, and there are few short cuts other than to leave your comfort zone and get yourself out there. One of the first bits of advice I give anyone who wants to make a difference in the world? It's to 'go out and make a difference in the world'. Find your passion first. The rest you can learn later – if and when you need it.

Each of the ten authors in this book did just that. And, in many cases, they weren't even aware that the particular problem they ended up experiencing – and fixing – even existed. In other words, the problem or solution found them. And that can only happen if you're somewhere it can find you. You won't, after all, get to experience 'Third World' maternal care in London, Paris or New York but you will if you follow Laura Stachel's lead and spend hard time on the ground in maternity wards in West Africa.

## THE MEANING OF RELUCTANCE

Given the nature of how Laura's innovation (and the nine others in this book) came about, you might be wondering why they're not accidental, or serendipitous, innovators. Why reluctant?

Over the past eighteen months, as this book gradually turned from idea to reality, everyone from publishers to authors to friends and colleagues have challenged my choice of the word 'reluctant'. Once or twice I was almost convinced to change it, but held firm. If the contents of this book generate anywhere near the level of debate that the title has, I'll be more than happy. The title is deliberately provocative, and I hope you get to experience reluctance in all its forms as you read each of the stories we've assembled here.

Some of the authors do prefer to call themselves 'accidental innovators', but I don't think this does justice to them or their story. I'd argue that it wasn't by accident that they found themselves in a situation that changed the course of their lives. Accident implies luck, but it wasn't luck that Laura Stachel found herself in Nigeria, or Sharon Terry's children were diagnosed with a genetic disorder, or Erik Hersman found himself deeply troubled by a crisis tearing his home country apart. I prefer the idea of reluctance, the idea that many of these people weren't looking for a cause to occupy their time or dominate their lives, and that in many cases they were fairly happy with everything before life got complicated. Sure, the rewards of a successful 'career' in social entrepreneurship can be significant if you stick to your path and fight like your life depends on it, but for all the romance of the discipline it is an often difficult, frustrating and lonely journey, and far from romantic. The very fact that someone would choose this path over one much easier to me also speaks of reluctance. The easy option isn't the one they took. They took the hard one for the greater good. You'll relive much of this pain, angst and frustration as you work your way through the pages of this book.

Reluctance also speaks of an awareness of that greater good, of a story and a cause bigger than any one person. Very few people would willingly put themselves in harms way – confront armed soldiers taking orders from a dictatorial president, for example. But activists do this around the world day after day, risking everything for a cause they believe in. They do it in pursuit of a bigger goal of freedom, for everyone. In an ideal world they wouldn't have to take those risks – the oppression and corruption wouldn't exist. But it does. Like them, many innovators reluctantly make their lives more dangerous, complex, frustrating or challenging for the bigger goal they chase. It's a decision they don't take lightly. For many, it's a considerable sacrifice, yet few would say no to a quieter, simpler life – one which all of them could likely have had. They're just not those kinds of people.

If one thing drives this home more than any other, it's family. While some people might dismiss their idea and continue as they were before, Sharon Terry, whose story you'll find in Chapter 9, had no such choice. Following a shock diagnosis that her children were suffering from a rare genetic disease about which very little was known, Sharon and her husband's lives turned in a completely new direction. Their reluctance was obvious. In her own words:

> As we fell asleep each night amid piles of photocopied papers and enormous medical dictionaries, we knew we had to take the bull by the horns. I remember an evening when we looked at each other, and thought, no, no, no – we don't want to do this – we do not want to create a system for this disease. Wasn't it enough to live with it, to cope with it, to walk our kids through it? Couldn't someone else make sense of it, fix it, give us a call when the cure was in? I begged the universe to please take care of us. No. Reluctantly, we had to admit that this was our burden. There was no one else.

Wes Janz, whose chapter closes the book, has his own take on the role of reluctance, arguing that what we need, in essence, is more of it. When faced with a problem, he gives this advice to budding social innovators:

> Don't do anything.
> Hesitate. Doubt. Be unsure. Be undecided.
> In other words, be reluctant.
> People determined to 'do something', or 'change the world' or 'make a difference' in someone else's life ... well, these folks scare me. Too often it is the case that the interventions of well-intentioned people are soon ignored by or bring harm to locals. Sometimes the best thing we can do for someone else (and ourselves) is to walk away. Let it be. Let them be.

# Doing the Right Thing in the Right Way

While we certainly want to encourage people to take an interest in helping others, we also need to make sure they go the right way about it, and do it respectfully. Wes's concern chimes closely with my own, where I frequently argue that we shouldn't develop solutions to problems we don't understand, that we shouldn't take ownership of a problem that isn't ours, and we certainly shouldn't build 'solutions' from thousands of miles away and then jump on a plane in search of a home for them. This, in the technology-for-development world I spend most of my time in these days, is generally what tends to happen. Good intentions, often poorly executed.

In a recent guest piece in the *Stanford Social Innovation Review*, I argued this very point. My argument was well received, but one commenter asked what I suggest all the people who lived far away from the problems of the developing world should do with their passion and time. My response was that there are problems everywhere, including where they lived, and it might be better to try and solve some of those instead. If people really do want to contribute to solving the problems of 'others' then they really need to go and live under the same conditions as them for a while. Each of the innovators in this book had exposure to the problems they decided to solve. I only felt remotely qualified to help grassroots non-profits in Africa with their communication problems because I'd spent the best part of twenty years living and working with them. It gave me an insight which was not only crucial to my solution working for them, but it also gave me credibility among the people I was trying to help.

# A Personal Journey

I've had my own share of reluctance, and difficulty, over the years. A cosy career in offshore banking beckoned at a young age, and while it promised to deliver materially, spiritually it felt far removed from the kinds of things I felt I should be doing. A trip to Zambia in 1993 changed everything, and exposed me to the realities of life for people much less fortunate than myself. And there were many. I soon realised that life sucked for 90% of people on the planet, and this deeply troubled me. It does to this day. Here was my call to action, but for longer than I remember I struggled to figure out precisely what that action should be. How could I personally contribute to fixing these huge, global injustices?

It's a question than can easily eat you up. I did get myself 'out there', though. I sold everything I owned on more than one occasion and left what I called home, a liberating experience as it turned out, even if it didn't feel that way at the time. I lived in places like Calabar, Southern Nigeria for a year running a primate sanctuary – twelve months in suffocating heat and humidity mixed with the odd bout of malaria. I'd often sit in my room at night with a candle, trying to capture my thoughts and frustrations in a diary, continually searching while drinking cheap Nigerian beer. As with much of the previous ten years, I didn't find anything.

It took a late night motorcycle accident on a busy Calabar road for my own particular life to turn. After eight days my leg was finally put back together in a hospital in Jersey, in the Channel Islands, where I was born. I lay there in pain with no money, no mobility, no job, nowhere to live and still no idea where my life was headed. This was the lowest I was to get. Soon after I received an unexpected phone call from an ex-colleague offering me work on a very early mobile-for-development project. I upped sticks once more and hobbled over to England to live. It was January 2003, ten years after my search began. Figuring out how mobile phones, still rare in number but rising quickly across the developing world, could help solve some of the more pressing conservation and development problems of our time was a perfect fit for me, blending my passion for technology with a passion for international development and a desire to help people solve their own problems.

FrontlineSMS, a text messaging communications platform today in use in over 150 countries around the world, was conceived two years later over a beer and a football match, and it quite literally saved me. I finally found purpose, an outlet for my passion and energy that I could believe in. The way people I had never met took it and did remarkable things for themselves and their communities genuinely inspired me, and kept me going during the many dark and challenging days ahead, particularly at the beginning. FrontlineSMS became my springboard, one which allowed me to move on and do other things I cared about. This book would not be here today without it, and perhaps neither would I.

The very real frustrations of life as a social innovator come alive on many of the pages of this book, and is testament to the great story-telling abilities of those who have contributed. But not all ventures end in success, and it would be wrong of this book to give that impression. Indeed, the social innovation graveyard is littered with ventures that either ran out of money, ran out of time, or ran out of ideas. The success-ful projects you read about here are among the few that didn't suffer that fate.

## Perspiration into Inspiration

When I started out there were few people I could turn to for advice and support, moral or otherwise. That's the price you pay, I suppose, for getting into something early. But things are different now – I found my purpose, threw everything at it, and came out the other side. I've learnt a lot along the way, and feel the least I can now do is help others who might be at the beginning of their own journey. Whether that be giving advice or a positive critique on an idea, a shot of encouragement, helping raise awareness through blog posts, giving tips on fundraising, making introductions to other projects and people with the same inter-ests, or offering to be a future soundboard as ideas grow and develop. These are all things I didn't have when I started out, and using them productively now that I do is one of the biggest contributions I believe I can – and should – make to the future growth of our discipline. This book is testament to that commitment.

Our legacy shouldn't be measured in the projects or tools we build – or, indeed, in the books that we write – but in the people we serve and inspire, and the future we help create.

In the social innovation world we talk a lot about project sustainabil-ity, but little about human sustainability. If we're to have any chance of ongoing success in our battle against the many problems facing society then we need to attract the brightest young minds to the field, and then give them all the support they need to keep them there. Empowerment isn't just something we do in a distant land. There's plenty we can be doing on our own doorstep. It's a different kind of empowerment, but that doesn't make it less valuable. If anything, it's more so.

## ADVICE FOR SOCIAL INNOVATORS AT HEART

I'll close as many of my fellow contributors have, and share a few lessons I've learnt as I stumbled my way through the world of social innovation. I hope some of these prove useful as you travel your own path.

- Ask yourself: do you really understand the problem you're trying to solve?
- Are you the best person to solve the problem? Be honest, and if not go and support the work of someone else who is.
- Don't be competitive. There's plenty of poverty to go around.
- Don't be in a hurry. Grow your idea or project on your own terms.
- Don't assume you need money to grow. Do what you can before you reach out to funders.
- Volunteers and interns may not be the silver bullet to your human resource issues. Finding people with your passion and commitment willing to work for free can be time consuming and challenging.
- Pursue and maximise every opportunity to promote your work. Be relentless.
- Suppress your ego. Stay humble. Remain curious.
- Remember that your website, for most people, is the primary window to you and your idea.
- Learn when to say 'no'. Manage expectations. Don't overstretch.
- Avoid being dragged down by the politics of the industry you're in. Save your energy for more important things.
- Learn to do what you can't afford to pay other people to do.
- Be open with the values that drive you. People will respect you for it.
- Collaborate if it's in the best interests of solving your problem, even if it's not in *your* best interests.

- Make full use of your networks, and remember that the benefits of being in them may not always be immediate.
- Remember the bigger picture, and that whatever you're trying to solve is bigger than any one person or organisation.
- Don't beat yourself up looking for your passion. You'll find it in the most unlikely of places, and if you don't it could very well find you.
- Finally, strive to be a good person, a role model for others. And if you do succeed, remember the importance of giving back.

Fuelled by the spread of the Internet and the ubiquity of mobile phones, there are more people working to solve pressing social and environmental problems in the world today than ever before in human history.

For anyone wanting to join them, it is my hope that *The Rise of the Reluctant Innovator* will show the way, or at least one way, and prove that the only qualifications you need to change the world are a little faith, hope and determination.

---

*Join the conversation online:*

**Twitter:**   @ReluctantsBook
**Facebook:**  facebook.com/ReluctantInnovation
**Website:**   reluctantinnovation.com

# 1

# LET A BILLION READERS BLOOM

## *Brij Kothari*

*Watching yet another Spanish movie in his friend's apartment to
avoid writing up his doctoral dissertation, Brij Kothari makes
a throwaway comment about subtitles, which plants the seed
of an idea and spawns a literacy initiative that has, in
Bill Clinton's words, 'a staggering impact on people's lives'.*

## CONCEPTION

What does *Women on the Verge of a Nervous Breakdown*, Pedro Almodóvar's zany award-winning film, have to do with mass literacy in India? Nothing, and yet ... everything! In early 1996, after almost a decade of student life at Cornell University in Ithaca, NY, I was finally in the home stretch of writing my doctoral dissertation. That is precisely when, I believe, the desire to watch movies peaks.

So there we were, Bernadette Joseph, my special friend at the time and now my wife, Chris Scott and his very pregnant wife, Stephanie

Buechler, watching this hysterical movie in Spanish at the Scott-Buechler apartment. As students of Spanish, we had soon discovered that watching movies in the language was not only effective, but also great fun. Those were pre-digital and pre-DVD days when foreign language movies in the USA came on videotapes with English language subtitles.

In an ambience of hilarity, a couple of unrelated thoughts crossed my mind during the movie. I wondered whether uncontrolled laughter could act like a natural Pitocin and precipitate labour. That one I had the good sense to keep to myself. The other thought, which I blurted out during a bathroom break, was simply: 'Why don't they put Spanish subtitles on Spanish films. We'd catch the dialogue better.' My friends agreed. So I casually ventured an extension, without worrying too much about its linguistic narrowness in a country that has 22 official languages and over a thousand dialects: 'Maybe India would become literate if they simply added Hindi lyrics to Hindi film songs.'

'I think you're onto something,' Chris reacted. Coming from a fluent Spanish and Hindi speaker who had grown up in India, who understood Bollywood's hold on Indian passions, it was the sort of nonchalant affirmation I needed in order for a synapse of an idea to become a lifelong obsession. The idea couldn't have had a more serendipitous beginning. But before I could get too excited about it, I had to confirm the originality of the thought. The idea seemed too ridiculously simple to have not been thought of, or tried, for mass literacy.

I found that most of the literature on subtitling was coming out of the USA and Western Europe. One major stream dealt with the use of subtitling for access to audio-visual content across languages or translation subtitling. Considerable attention is devoted to how translation subtitling can and does contribute to additional language acquisition (second, third, foreign, and so on). Some even suggested subtitling in the 'same' language for improving one's pronunciation and listening comprehension. The other major stream, Closed-Captioning (CC), leveraged subtitling for media access among the deaf and hearing impaired. A trickle of articles talked about subtitling as karaoke in the limited context of entertainment in bars or on increasingly popular home-based karaoke machines.

The bulk of the literature made one crucial assumption; subtitling was only for functionally literate viewers. Still, there was an occasional mention of the potential of subtitling to support reading skill development, lost in the cacophony of subtitling for other purposes. The idea of 'same' language subtitling was articulated in some cases with academic terms like 'unilingual', 'intralingual' and 'bimodal' subtitles, in the context of language acquisition. The odd piece, however, would also refer to subtitling and its potential for literacy. Subtitling in the 'same' language for literacy, albeit in a limited classroom or research context, had at least found a passing expression.

It would be fair to ask about the original contribution we were making. The first thing that occurred to me was that the idea of 'sameness' tying audio and text was somehow lost in the many monikers floating around in the literature, like, unilingual, intralingual and bimodal subtitling. The tight bond I wanted to forge between audio and subtitles needed a more fitting term that brought 'sameness' of language front and centre. The term 'Same Language Subtitling', and its very own acronym (SLS), thus came into being.

Concocting SLS felt a bit like sweet revenge for all the academic jargon I had endured in my coursework in graduate school. Now I had my own term to inflict upon others. My literature review made two things patently clear. SLS had never been used on television or other mass audio-visual media, anywhere in the world, expressly for the purpose of improving mass reading or literacy skills among functional non-literates. Research on the potential impact of SLS exposure, or subtitling generally, on the reading skills of early-readers, was rare. To an aspiring academic trained in development communication and education, stumbling upon a novel idea, as yet unproven, at the crossroads of these two fields, felt tantamount to finding the proverbial pot of gold.

By the time I had finished writing my dissertation, 'Towards a Praxis of Oppressed Local Knowledges: Participatory Ethnobotanical Research in Indigenous Communities of Ecuador', a mouthful that couldn't be further from subtitling and literacy, I had been offered a faculty position at the Indian Institute of Management, Ahmedabad (IIMA), in its Ravi J. Matthai Centre for Educational Innovation. The centre was created in honour of IIMA's first full-time Director who had a vision of establishing an institute of management dedicated to the application of management principles, not just to business, but also to the public and social sectors. Although I did not realise at the time, SLS could not have found a more suitable base than here at one of India's most prestigious institutes. The year was 1996. Within nine months, SLS would go from conception in a living room in the USA to its first tiny steps in India.

## LIFE BEFORE SLS

While most of the SLS story developed in India after 1996, it would be remiss of me not to outline the part played previously by the Sri Auro-bindo Ashram, the Indian Institute of Technology (IIT Kanpur), Cornell University and Ecuador in shaping my abilities, interests and motivations to pursue this idea.

I had the fortune to grow up from ages of six to twenty, literally in one long sweep, at the Sri Aurobindo Ashram in Pondicherry, India, entirely schooled at its Sri Aurobindo International Centre of Education (SAICE). In a country where fierce educational competition and specialisation is the norm, it was unusual to experience an 'integral' system that aimed for a broad-based education, including a strong emphasis on languages, literature, performance arts, music and especially a physical and spiritual education. The medium of instruction was English and French. Every student picked up an average of three other Indian languages and had considerable flexibility to choose subjects, teachers and even the time one wished to allot to particular subjects. There were no exams, from kindergarten to college, and therefore no degree(s) to boot. The guiding philosophy was to awaken a love for learning built on the precept that every life has a higher transformational purpose. I grew up with a strong belief that if I could contribute to human progress in any meaningful way, I would be happy to have lived up to the ideals of SAICE, an institution that is at the core of shaping my identity.

The first exam I ever took was at the Master's level in physics, at IIT Kanpur, arguably the pinnacle of competition in India. How a degree-less student got into IIT Kanpur is another story, but once I was there a two-year stint allowed me to acquire my first real degree and join the educational mainstream. It also humbled me by bringing me face to face with some sharp minds and a timely realisation that it would have been a loss to physics had I continued any further in the field. Nevertheless, that degree served as a launch pad for my dream of studying in the USA. Fortunately, Cornell accepted me for a Masters degree, but this time in communication. I could safely decline a couple of other acceptances I had for an onward PhD in physics. As my train changed tracks, little did I fathom that it would be for a decade-long sojourn in Ithaca, NY.

More than any other place, Cornell brought to bear a focused desire for international development, through two years in the department of communication followed by eight more in education. It was stimulating to be around student colleagues, many of whom I encountered in cross-departmental courses, cafeterias and graduate student parties, who not only spoke eloquently about how to change the world, but also had clear-headed strategies to achieve their goals. You just had to catch them early enough in the party. People were dazzlingly adept at making connections between seemingly disparate ideas, which sometimes provided great comic relief, but often produced 'eureka' moments.

I realise now that I must thrive on serendipity. The topic for my doctoral research came to me initially in the form of a $99 coupon from Continental Airlines (now part of United Airlines) for a round trip from anywhere in the USA to Ecuador. My trip started as an opportunity to see Ecuador, Peru and Bolivia. A chance encounter in a Sunday market with Mr Juan José Simbaña, the president of an organisation representing seven communities in Andean Ecuador, led to a two-year immersion in Imbabura province. Simbaña and his people were concerned about conserving their knowledge of medicinal plants. I was enamoured with participatory action research. Together we conceived and executed, with two campesino volunteers from every community as co-researchers, one man and one woman, a project to document their knowledge of medicinal plants, for themselves.

Although all campesinos selected as co-researchers were literate, the majority of their own community members, for whom they were documenting their knowledge, were not. Low literacy achievement in rural schools further exacerbated the problem of how to conserve knowledge in the absence of basic functional literacy. To bridge the literacy gap, we decided to represent every medicinal plant and its administration visually. We devised an icon-based representation of medicinal plant preparation and usage, resulting in the publication of a bilingual, Quichua–Spanish book, *Ñucanchic Panpa Janpicuna: Plantas Medicinales del Campo, Abya-Yala, Quito,* in 1993.

My dissertation documented the entire action research process, including a critique of extractive forms of ethnobotanical research among indigenous peoples. While watching Pedro Almodóvar's movie that winter night in Ithaca, NY, my thinking was already a ferment of Paulo Freire and his approach to literacy, Bob Marley and his songs of freedom, and a new-found passion for Spanish and Latin America. Subtitling Bollywood songs for mass literacy was hardly a stretch. That same year, in September 1996, I accepted IIM Ahmedabad's offer, the first and only real job I've ever had.

## SLS: The First Five Years (1997–2001)

As a new arrival, my immediate motivation was to publish and get tenure. So I began putting together a research agenda based around SLS. The early hitch was that I was in an institute of management, albeit within a centre for educational innovation. Admittedly, this is my reading of the situation. At least some of my faculty colleagues valued a research focus on innovation in educational management, with the focus on 'management'. My proposed research was at the intersection of literacy and media. I credit the academic freedom of the institute and some faculty colleagues who encouraged me to pursue any direction of research that seemed meaningful to me and not be overly preoccupied with undercurrents that would rather see me fit in.

After crudely subtitling some Gujarati film songs, in Gujarati, at a local videographer's studio that specialised in covering weddings, we set out to test receptivity to SLS among our target viewers. In villages and slums, at train stations and bus stops, wherever it was easy enough for curiosity to gather a crowd, our small research team would set up two identical TV sets, connected to VCRs, synchronously playing the same film songs. One showed the songs with SLS, the other without. The onlookers' reactions were recorded on video.

*Author interacting with viewers in Gulbai Tekra Slum, Ahmedabad (2002). Photo courtesy of Jaydeep Bhatt, © PlanetRead.*

Everywhere, it quickly became clear that most viewers – literates and weak-literates alike, children, youth and adults – preferred songs with SLS. Surveys later confirmed that around 90% preferred SLS. The top-of-mind reason was usually that SLS enhanced the entertainment value of songs, although around 20% also mentioned that it was good for literacy. The karaoke effect is what viewers enjoy foremost, including the ability to sing along, and know the song lyrics. A majority of non-literates wanted SLS, not because it was beneficial for them, but because it was perceived to be good for children in their family and social networks. Some also saw in SLS the primary benefit that is attributed to closed-captioning – media access among the hearing impaired, to which one might also add improved access to the audio in a strident Indian television viewing context characterised by group conversations and ambient noise.

A few who did not prefer SLS seemed not to mind living with it. In other words, SLS did not provoke a strong rejection. For the literates in this camp, SLS had nothing special to offer and, if anything, served as a distraction from the visuals. The karaoke benefit was insufficient to offset the diversionary effect of SLS. Fortunately, though, most literates also took to SLS. We were aware all along that the idea, even though it was targeting the weak-literates, could not succeed on mainstream television without also winning over the literates. In the long run, it had to be established that SLS did not hurt ratings and, ideally, improved them.

The overwhelming preference we found for SLS was a necessary first step, but did it lead to automatic reading engagement? To explore this question we bought an eye-tracker that, once calibrated, could tell us, 60 times per second, where exactly a viewer was focusing on the screen. The focal points, when plotted, paint an accurate pattern of a viewer's eye movement. We brought into our lab several weak-literates, showing the same person a film song, first without and then with SLS. Unlike the standard Bollywood song without SLS, the resulting focal pattern from a song with SLS had two distinct bands. The bottom band visually and precisely captured viewer engagement with the subtitles. SLS was evidently not being ignored by the weak-literates, an observation consistent with a similar finding by the highly respected Belgian professor, Géry d'Ydewalle, whose ground breaking research on subtitling was undertaken predominantly with literates. Whereas he concluded that, if the subtitles are there they will be read by literates, our conclusion with weak-literates, at best, could be that if subtitles are there, they will be attended to.

The eye-movement pattern alone did not allow us to ascribe reading engagement, let alone reading improvement. A noteworthy weakness of our eye-tracking research was its artificiality. The weak-literate viewers, already edgy from being in an institutional lab, had to position themselves on a chin and head support and undergo a process of instrumental calibration before actual data collection could begin. The instrumentation required that only the eyes could move while viewing. Overall, it was a far cry from enjoying film songs on TV at home. Still, it brought us another small step closer to proving the scientific merit of SLS. Weak-literates, like literates, simply could not and would not ignore SLS.

Through qualitative interviews captured on video in the villages and slums of Gujarat state, we determined that people claimed not merely to look at the subtitle band, but also to try to read along. The popularity of SLS, and the fact that people were attending to it and asserting that it was inviting reader engagement, were expected to result in measurable improvement of reading skills.

Our first real study on the impact of SLS was conducted in 1998/99 in a municipal school in Ahmedabad, serving low-income children. Half the students in grades 3 and 4, the stage at which the Hindi language is introduced in such schools, were regularly exposed to Hindi songs with SLS. The other half saw the same songs, but without SLS. After three months of exposure, three times a week for roughly 30 minutes in each session, we found that the SLS group was, measurably, further along in reading Hindi. This was the first real piece of evidence that SLS had a positive impact on reading skills. Arguably, however, the value of SLS had been found in a controlled setting wherein students were artificially and regularly required to watch songs with SLS. Nevertheless, that study laid the groundwork for piloting SLS on mainstream television. With that began the protracted battles for mindsets. At the time, we had only a vague presentiment that it would take more than research and data to move people with decision-making power.

Armed with the study and videos of people's reactions to SLS, I wrote to all the directors of state television networks, known as Doordarshan Kendras (DDKs), and several private channels, seeking permission to try out SLS on an existing song-based TV programme. Doordarshan (DD) is India's national/state television network. The only reply I received from state regional channels was from a Mr Satish Saxena, who appreciated the idea. His only regret was that he was the Director of All India Radio (AIR) and not television.

To my surprise, private channels did not pick up on the idea either. Our proposal that SLS would not hurt their programming, and if anything help it a bit, did not cut ice, even if it meant the nation would benefit substantially in terms of literacy. Private channels were very clear – they wanted to be paid for allowing SLS because their medium was contributing to literacy. Not only would the SLS project have to raise funds to cover the cost of SLS, it would have to implement SLS and pay the channel handsomely for permitting SLS. Literacy was clearly not on the agenda of the several private channels I contacted. The state seemed a better bet. DD is a public service broadcaster and historically has had a greater proportion of weak-reading and low-income viewers in rural India, although this is changing with increasing penetration of private networks.

I met seven of the DDK directors personally, in Jaipur, Trivandrum, Chennai, Mumbai, Hyderabad, Bangalore and Ahmedabad. They were all certain that SLS would detract from the entertainment value of song programmes. Video testimonies and surveys to the contrary, whenever it was possible to share, did not persuade them otherwise. SLS was rejected based on a personal hunch that viewers would not like this 'intrusion'. Close to my institute, the then Director of DDK Ahmedabad rejected SLS, too. When I requested that he see the video testimonies, he refused, citing years of experience and understanding of what viewers would or would not like. In Mumbai, a private producer of a popular film song programme, Chitrahaar, similarly rejected SLS saying that he was convinced it would be a distraction. I discovered early on that data were necessary, but clearly not sufficient in themselves to dislodge strong convictions, especially among people with power.

Then something fortuitous happened. DDK Ahmedabad appointed a new Director, the same Mr Satish Saxena. He agreed to allow SLS on four episodes of a Gujarati film song programme, Chitrageet. Letters of support came in from several viewers. Mr Saxena directly received congratulatory messages for the wonderful work he had initiated for literacy. So he agreed to allow SLS on Chitrageet, as long as it was a free service to DDK Ahmedabad. The challenge then became financial. We had to find the necessary funds to keep SLS on air for at least one year, long enough to conduct a meaningful research study on the impact of SLS on literacy.

The scramble to fund the first ever SLS pilot on mainstream television, for mass literacy, led me to Mr B. S. Bhatia, Director of the Development and Communication Unit (DECU) at the Indian Space Research Organisation (ISRO) in Ahmedabad. He also happened to be an IIM Ahmedabad alumnus. In a timely manner, he came up with the necessary funds to continue SLS on Chitrageet for one year, making it possible to conduct a proper baseline and impact study. The impact results of the first TV pilot were again positive and compared well with the earlier school experiment's findings. The evidence was available as early as 2000 that SLS on film songs on broadcast television contributed positively to reading skills.

Naturally we approached the National Literacy Mission (NLM) to consider SLS for scale up and financial support. The NLM referred the matter to an internal expert who, in essence, gave an opinion that it was not a new idea and, by implication, a tried and failed one. There was no dialogue about where, when and by whom anything like SLS had been implemented for mass reading. Having worked on SLS since 1996 and scoured the literature on subtitling and its uses in education, I could say then, and still maintain now, that the expert's opinion was just that – an opinion, not supported by evidence. Nevertheless, it had the effect of setting back my conversation with the NLM and its parent Ministry of Human Resource Development (MHRD) by several years.

Unable to find a toehold in education, I decided to approach broadcasting. Backed by research evidence and the fact that viewers in Gujarat had responded positively to SLS on DDK Ahmedabad, I approached Doordarshan (DD) Directorate in New Delhi. A Deputy Director General there heard me out patiently. A few weeks later, a brief letter informed me summarily that DD had reviewed our tapes and were not interested in SLS. No reason was provided. It did not matter that SLS had just had a successful run on DDK Ahmedabad, one of DD's own regional channels.

## SLS: THE SECOND FIVE YEARS (2002–2006)

The strategy and challenge for the SLS project became one of achieving international recognition in order to overcome domestic indifference. As happens sometimes in India, our policy makers are swayed more by international credibility than the intrinsic merit of an innovation. In early 2002, the SLS innovation proposed by IIM Ahmedabad won the top prize at a global innovation competition, 'Development Marketplace' (DM), conducted at the World Bank in Washington, DC. The honour came with a grant of $250,000 to take SLS forward, the top award possible that year under the rules of the competition. The President of the World Bank, Sir James Wolfensohn, was chaperoned to our display booth before the award ceremony. That award changed the DD Directorate's perspective on SLS.

The DM success made it possible to approach the Director General of DD, Dr S. Y. Quraishi. At my request, the Director of IIM Ahmedabad, Professor Jahar Saha, flew in with me for this meeting in New Delhi. Dr Quraishi was quick to recognise the potential of SLS and immediately gave permission for one year of SLS on Chitrahaar, one of the longest running, nationally telecast programme of Hindi film songs. This was a breakthrough moment.

Lower down the DD hierarchy, however, a peculiar challenge emerged despite Dr Quraishi's approval at the top. One of the directors given charge of handling the SLS project laid down one strict condition. IIM Ahmedabad would be allowed to add SLS for a year, after which the expensive broadcast editing equipment, paid for by the DM (World Bank) grant, and therefore belonging to my institution, would have to be handed over to DD. We suggested that might be possible if DD agreed to continue SLS on Chitrahaar, or an equivalent programme, for an additional two years. This resulted in a stalemate that nearly derailed our efforts even to start SLS on Chitrahaar. The DM grant was at risk of lapsing. Six months into the one-year grant, the matter came to Dr Quraishi's attention and he overruled the director's condition. He agreed, as we had been arguing all along, that it was not appropriate to lay claim on equipment acquired by IIM Ahmedabad, paid for by an international grant to the institution.

With permissions in place, SLS was implemented on Chitrahaar for one year, starting in September 2002. As a requirement of the DM grant, data for the baseline and impact studies were independently collected from four Hindi speaking states and Gujarat, by ORG-Centre for Social Research. The sample was composed of randomly selected weak-reading and non-literate people in TV-owning households. The identical battery of tests to measure reading and writing skills were administered to the exact same individuals, first at baseline and then a year later. In the interim, SLS was implemented on Chitrahaar. The surveys captured the regularity of viewing Chitrahaar. The analysis compared reading and writing skill improvement among those who watched Chitrahaar regularly with those who did not.

*Still from Jodhaa Akbar with Same Language Subtitling. © Disney UTV.*

Like the previous two studies, we found yet again that SLS exposure improved reading skills. The impact size, as expected, was small, in view of the short period of implementation and possible exposure in broadcast mode, but it was measurable and statistically significant. We concluded that SLS did cause reading skills to be practised, on a mass scale. More than a year's exposure was probably required to convert the average viewer from weak-reading to functional reading ability. How much longer? That was the question we tackled next. A baseline of reading skills across Hindi speaking states was already in place. We just had to keep SLS alive on TV in the same states, long enough to re-visit our baseline sample. This was mostly a financial challenge, but not without its moments of political angst.

Buoyed by the international recognition of DM and the partnership forged with DD to implement SLS on a national programme in Hindi, I approached the then Union Minister for Information and Broadcasting for a meeting to see whether SLS could be scaled up through her ministry. To my surprise, I secured a meeting rather easily. As soon as I began showing her a Hindi film song with Hindi subtitles, and before I could present our research findings or reveal that a sample programme with SLS was already on air, she cut me off, saying: 'I don't think this can have any impact on literacy.' Her secretary immediately took the cue and called in the next person while showing me the door. Less than a minute into the meeting, the Minister's opinion from the gut had pre-empted any further discussion of the thinking, research or experience backing the innovation. It was my first brush with raw power and its ability to quash ideas. I didn't dare mention that SLS was already on TV for fear that a phone call from her might kill whatever progress we had made over the years with DD. Fortunately that phone call was never made. I recall my elation when I read in the news a few weeks later that a cabinet reshuffle had resulted in the Minister being given a different portfolio.

From 2003 to date we have been able to keep SLS running, not on Chitrahaar, but Rangoli, a weekly one-hour programme of Hindi film songs, telecast nationally. Between 2003 and 2006 the SLS project was able to stretch DM support and buttress it with three separate research grants from MHRD, each made possible by a different Union Secretary overseeing the Department of Elementary Education and Literacy. MHRD seemed to be slowly warming up to SLS at the highest levels of bureaucracy.

On the broadcasting side, I approached Mr K. S. Sarma, CEO of the Broadcasting Corporation of India, better known as Prasar Bharati (PB). PB is an autonomous body that sets policy for television and radio nationally. I learned that Mr Sarma was visiting DDK Mumbai on official duty, so I put in a word with the DDK director there for a meeting but received word that I could not be accommodated. Feeling like a member of the paparazzi, I waited at the exit from his conference room. The CEO emerged finally at the end of the day, with a retinue of officials in tow, and walked straight to a car waiting outside. I introduced myself as a member of the faculty of IIM Ahmedabad and requested a couple of minutes to share details of an innovation. He was in a rush, but said that I could ride with him to his hotel. I discovered, that day, a rare benefit of Mumbai traffic jams.

Mr Sarma saw my laptop presentation in his car with great patience and interest. By the end of the ride, he had suggested that SLS could also be tried in regional languages and on the songs in feature films, not just on song programmes like Chitrahaar and Rangoli. This latter suggestion turned out to be a better solution from a couple of perspectives. Feature films attract on average four times the viewership of song programmes, and the songs therein are easier to subtitle. This is because song-based programmes are prone to last-minute decision making on what is to be included. Films are not. I imagine a phone call from Mr Sarma is all it took for us to begin SLS on the songs of the Telugu feature films on DDK Hyderabad. Both Dr Quraishi's and Mr Sarma's support at the helm of DD and PB set the tone for people lower down the broadcasting bureaucracy, and others who stepped into their shoes later, to allow SLS on more programmes and for years to come. The only condition was that SLS had to be kept on air at zero cost to the broadcaster.

In August of 2003, I was awarded a one-year fellowship to join the Reuters Digital Vision Program (RDVP) at Stanford University. One of my concrete goals alongside the fellowship was to set up a legal mechanism in the USA to receive US charitable contributions for SLS work. The RDVP and Stanford connections put me in touch with Scott Smith, then a lawyer at Bingham & McCutchen in San Francisco. By the time my fellowship ended, they had set up PlanetRead (US) as a non-profit, free of charge. With PlanetRead (US) in place we quickly set up Planet-Read (India), another non-profit based in Pondicherry, India, so that funds could pass between them to support work in India.

The entrepreneurial spirit at Stanford inspired me to participate in the 'Social e-Challenge' a business plan competition on campus. Our team of four undergraduates won that year. We additionally roped in Stuart Gannes, the Director of RDVP, to co-found BookBox, Inc., a social venture that produces animated stories for children in many languages, using SLS. But that's another story. Immediately following RDVP completion, Ashoka stepped in to offer a fellowship. As any Ashoka fellow knows, the fellowship came at a critical time, allowing me to throw caution to the wind and focus 100% on SLS.

During my RDVP days, I had occasion to present our SLS work at several conferences in the bay area, including at UC Berkeley and Stanford. Somewhere in those presentations SLS caught the imagination of someone at the then recently formed Google Foundation (GF). It was a slightly surreal moment when someone from GF called me to ask whether the SLS project might be interested in receiving some funding. Conversations relating to funding generally move in the opposite direction, so I found it impossible to explain to others hoping for GF support exactly how PlanetRead, a little known entity at the time, had swung it. PlanetRead (US) received $350,000 over two years to scale up SLS on eight weekly TV programmes in India, in as many languages.

Immediately, we confronted another challenge. PlanetRead (India) could not receive foreign currency from any entity without what is known as a permission under the Foreign Currency Regulation Act (FCRA). Securing a one-time clearance for transfer of funds was relatively easy, so we did that first. We were told, however, that a 'permanent' FCRA permit for PlanetRead (India) would exact an unofficial price, which we were not willing to pay, on principle. After many follow-up trips to the FCRA office in New Delhi, often requiring me to deal with minor technicalities that the officers were clearly using to delay granting of FCRA clearance in the hope of extracting something more meaningful, we finally prevailed. As on so many previous occasions, membership of the faculty at IIM Ahmedabad ultimately helped me to succeed. Nevertheless, I couldn't help but calculate which was costlier – paying for the many trips to New Delhi or paying the unofficial rate. The latter would have been cheaper, purely in financial terms, if the cost of a compromised conscience were not factored in.

## SLS: THE THIRD FIVE YEARS (2007–2011)

Part of the funding we received from GF was for measuring the impact of SLS, after five years of exposure, by revisiting our 2002 baseline sample in 2007. The study was again commissioned to Nielsen's ORG-CSR. The results this time were more than encouraging. Regular SLS exposure from Class 1-5 was found to more than double the rate of functional readers in Class 5 and halve the rather high rate of complete illiteracy also found in Class 5. SLS exposure was found to raise the rate of newspaper reading among 'literate' youth from 34% to 70%. Many so-called literate youths, who were actually functionally illiterate, had reading practice with SLS and, over time, became functionally literate and picked up newspapers. We concluded from this study that it took anywhere from three to five years of one-hour-per-week exposure to SLS for most weak-literates to progress from weak-literacy to functional literacy. Of course, further research would reveal whether daily exposure could shorten the period further.

Since the time of the 2006 GF grant, PlanetRead and IIM Ahmedabad's strategy has been to maintain SLS on eight to ten weekly TV programmes in as many languages, in the belief that it provides an effective national cover from under which to influence policy. Maintenance of SLS at this level has not been easy. Our experience has been that every major funder who has supported PlanetRead has done so for around two years. That includes, in chronological order, Development Marketplace, the Google Foundation, Sir Ratan Tata Trust and Dell Giving. Our horizon of funding assurance has never really extended much beyond one year. At least a couple of times the SLS project has come critically close to shutting down for lack of resources, but somehow one thing or another has always come through, sometimes from unexpected sources. Since 2008, for example, an anonymous donor has been sending, through an intermediary, an annual cheque for up to $50,000. Thank you, anonymous donor, for this highly valuable unrestricted support, which allows PlanetRead to push SLS in policy and raise the idea's profile internationally. Almost all the other funding PlanetRead has received so far has been for specific projects.

Over the years, our SLS operations have been streamlined to a point where getting tapes from channels, subtitling them without any spelling errors and sending them back to the broadcaster is the least of our challenges. That aspect of our work tends to run efficiently on autopilot. Other than maintaining a steady fund flow, our biggest challenge is without doubt convincing transient policy makers to support and take ownership of SLS long enough to advance it in policy, within the limited window of opportunity presented by their short tenures in specific positions. Building institutional memory of the progress has never been easy in a situation where one senior officer's decision in a position of power is easily supplanted by the next, while everyone below in the hierarchy tends to tow the line.

In our case, the support of three successive Union Secretaries at MHRD was neutralised easily by subsequent secretaries. After the SLS project enjoyed support from Union Secretaries Mr M. K. Kaw, Mr Kumud Bansal and Champak Chaterjee while they were at the helm of MHRD, it entered a phase where it was difficult to find any clear support from officers in similarly high positions. Since 2004 my interactions with Union Secretaries and Joint Secretaries serving as the DG of NLM have remained either neutral, meaning that I could not read their position, or in some cases clearly unsympathetic.

My second ministerial encounter was on August 11th, 2009, again with the Union Minister of Information & Broadcasting (MI&B). This time, however, it was a different Minister, Ms Ambika Soni. In contrast to my earlier meeting with the previous Minister, this one went much better. She heard me out patiently and was quick to appreciate the value of SLS. As soon as I finished my presentation, she called in her Personal Assistant, and explained to him what we were doing. It was clear that she had grasped the concept. She then asked me about the budget to scale it up nationally. I told her that it would be around $1 million annually, to scale up on fifty weekly programmes. She told her PA that since it was DD's commemorative year – it had just completed fifty years – she could think of considering SLS as a part of that.

Minister Soni asked me to follow up with the then DG at DD. The next day I was in the DG's office. Her entire tone was one of action, giving me a feeling that a message might have gone to her from the Minister's office. Upon the DG's request, a proposal was sent to her, with a copy to the Minister. To cut a long story short, I received a letter from the Minister's office several months later to the effect that, while SLS was a good idea, there were no funds to support the proposal for a national scale up. What seemed like a window of opportunity in policy was once again proving to be a glass ceiling.

In 2009, I was invited to the Clinton Global Initiative (CGI) where Bill Clinton personally endorsed SLS in a plenary session. The video of his endorsement has become the most powerful tool we have to enhance the credibility of SLS. India's Union Minister of State, MHRD, responsible for literacy, was present in the audience and met me at CGI subsequently. At her suggestion, I followed up with a meeting in New

Delhi, growing increasingly confident that SLS was close to acceptance in MHRD policy. In October 2009 the DG NLM invited me to present to a committee. At his request, I sent him yet another proposal for a national scale up.

The next month, I was asked to present to the Union Minister, MHRD and senior MHRD officials, including the Secretary, DG NLM and other senior officers. My presentation was the last one in a series that day. Before I could start, the Minister said: 'Tell me what you're going to tell me.' Sensing that he might be in a rush, I offered to cut my presentation to five minutes, down from the allocation of 15 minutes. The Minister simply reiterated: 'No. Tell me what you're going to tell me.' So I simply told him that my presentation was on SLS, an innovation that could potentially deliver regular reading practice to over 300 million weak-literates in India, if implemented widely on television. He shot back: 'This has nothing to do with literacy. You should talk to some other Ministry.'

I suggested that he just see a small clip of a song with SLS. By then he had already made up his mind and had turned to his cadre of senior officers to move to the next agenda item. I had no choice but to leave the conference room, no doubt feeling crushed and left wondering, even today, what it was that made him slam the door so hard on an innovation backed by over a decade of research and development, at one of the country's most prestigious institutions? SLS had by then won many international honours and had been presented at conferences in some of the world's most prestigious universities such as UC Berkeley and Stanford. How does one fathom that it could be dismissed as 'nothing to do with literacy' in less time than it takes Usain Bolt to run the 100 metres?

The same month, the Schwab Foundation and United Nations Development Programme (UNDP) gave me the Indian Social Entrepreneur of the Year Award for 2009 at the India Economic Forum. As a Schwab social entrepreneur the World Economic Forum (WEF) network – including Davos – became accessible to me. At the following year's award ceremony the chief guest happened to be the same Union Minister. I approached him after the day's events to see whether the conversation on SLS could be restarted. He looked at me, then my business card, and walked away. If I had not realised it earlier, it was now patently clear that SLS had gone from a potentially soaring priority at MHRD to dropping off a cliff.

A month later UNESCO invited me to CONFINTEA VI in Brazil, an International Conference on Adult Education. CONFINTEA is an intergovernmental conference on literacy that takes place every twelve to thirteen years and is attended by delegations from over 100 countries. There again, I met the Indian Union Minister of State, MHRD responsible for literacy, who had also seen SLS featured by Bill Clinton at CGI. She was accompanied by DG, NLM who said that he would put the SLS proposal 'back on track' especially given the earlier non-starter with the Union Minister. That was four years ago. Clearly, nobody is likely to touch SLS at MHRD until a new Union Minister takes over.

With no headway in sight at MHRD, I decided to turn my attention to broadcasting policy. In June 2010, I met the recently appointed Chairperson of the Prasar Bharati (PB) Board, a respected journalist, Ms Mrinal Pande. In most policy interactions, the power differential is quickly made apparent. This was different and felt like a conversation between mutually respectful professionals. At the end of the meeting she suggested that I write a formal letter to her requesting a presentation to the PB Board. Less than a month later I had met the Chairperson, and a presentation on SLS was on the agenda.

In July 2010, I made a ten-minute presentation to the full PB Board. During the interactions it was obvious that the board had appreciated the SLS concept and the research supporting the innovation. A question was raised on whether SLS might hurt the ratings. It was answered by another board member, who said what I would have said: that it actually works the other way. SLS contributes to ratings by 10–15%. For the first time, SLS was recorded in policy as an innovation with potential that the executive arm, namely DD, could consider taking forward.

Meanwhile, in February 2011, the National Association of Software and Services Companies (NASSCOM) Foundation selected SLS for the NASSCOM Social Innovation Honours for 2011. Ironically, the chief guest who gave away the honours happened to be none other than the Union Minister, MHRD who had earlier dismissed SLS as having nothing to do with literacy. Of course, the real award would have been if he had suggested that I meet him some time to present our work. That did not happen, even though national literacy does come squarely under his Ministry. In the media glare of flash photographers and video, not to mention several hundred conference delegates, he simply said: 'Good work. Keep it up.' I don't think he ever changed his mind on whether SLS had anything to do with literacy.

More than three years have passed since my presentation to the PB Board. The first two years saw nothing but turmoil for PB. Several complications arose from the handling of the broadcasting rights for the Commonwealth Games. A Presidential reference followed by a Supreme Court directive led to the suspension of a CEO of PB. The DG, DD at the time was unceremoniously sent back to her state.

## Is This the Last Mile?

In August 2011, after a considerable gap, finally a new DG, DD was appointed. I met Mr Tripurari Sharan literally a couple of days after his appointment, to restart the SLS conversation and hand him a proposal for a national scale up. Soon after, in February 2012, a new CEO, PB, Mr Jawhar Sircar, was also appointed. They both expressed a willingness to take SLS forward in policy, and they have.

Mr Sharan continues to demonstrate the same high level of pro-activity and enthusiasm for SLS that Dr Quraishi once did in the same position. In what I see as a highly atypical move by a senior bureaucrat, Mr Sharan immediately opened up several channels of communication with me, the most significant being email and mobile. He wrote to the Planning Commission (PC) requesting a special fund allocation for SLS, given that it is an innovation and, therefore, not easily accommodated under existing budgetary heads.

Mr Montek Singh Ahluwalia, the Deputy Chairman, PC, who reports directly to the Prime Minister (Chairman, PC), wrote in response – and I paraphrase slightly – that Same Language Subtitling is an important literacy initiative that should be supported as a Central Sector Scheme as and when posed by the Department. Somewhat ambiguous, perhaps, but it is the strongest policy endorsement yet for SLS, not least because of who it came from.

It took six months to understand and meet the 'as and when posed by the Department' condition. DD put up its own proposal on SLS to MI&B. MI&B raised certain queries. DD responded to those queries. Ultimately, MI&B sent DD's SLS proposal to PC. Too many acronyms, I know, but they underline the protracted nature of the process.

That is the policy story so far, poised at a high point of hope. We wait with bated breath for PC, under the leadership of Mr Ahluwalia, to make a final decision on whether to provide financial support for a national scale-up of SLS on fifty weekly programmes, for five years.

Alongside the policy story, we continue to win competitions, funds and attention, enabling us to keep SLS, now well into its teens, alive and growing. There have been some recent non-policy victories. In September 2012, we won the All Children Reading Grand Challenge, run by USAID, to scale up SLS in Maharashtra state. At Davos in 2013, Gordon Brown – the UN Special Envoy for Global Education – took some time out to understand SLS and has been referring to it in sound bites ever since. Policy in India, and perhaps other parts of the world, may slowly be waking up to the potential of SLS on TV for mass literacy.

## ACKNOWLEDGEMENTS

The pursuit of a social innovation often requires a heavy dose of irrationality. I am eternally obliged to Burny, Azul, Akash and Tara for accepting my madness with grace.

# 2

## SILICON SAVANNAH RISING

# Erik Hersman

*Worried about the political turmoil in Kenya, and concerned
at the lack of information forthcoming from his adoptive
country, Erik Hersman mobilises his own five-strong army
to conceive, create and launch a web-based facility that
revolutionises how breaking news is disseminated worldwide.*

## MY WORK IN CONTEXT

The air is cool and smells with the scent that seems only to come
from airplanes and dry cleaners. A dotted red line shows our path
for the next seven hours. And I find myself fortunate today as I sit in an
exit row, so the computer can actually fit on my lap without banging up
against the seat in front of me.

Soon I'll land in London. There I'll navigate meetings with top executives in some of the world's largest tech companies. There I'll stand
on a stage and speak to a couple hundred people about Africa. There

I'll find the funding for my endeavours. When I land back in Kenya in three days I'll take meetings with local start-up entrepreneurs, enjoy cheering while I attend the large annual sevens rugby tournament, all while weaving my motorcycle between the cars jamming up the city.

## What Allows Me to Handle Both Worlds?

Thirty-six thousand feet below us is the land where I spent my youngest years. We're crossing over that border point, a nebulous region from above, where South Sudan, Kenya and Uganda butt up against each other. A place where a murky memory serves up images of dusty roads, a metal mabati house in the bush, lost toys in the sand river, escape from flash floods with my sister, hunting lizards, and my village dog and tiny antelope pets.

My memory flashes forward to urban Nairobi of the 1980s, right after the coup. Of soccer fields, tinkering with small electrical engines, towels draped like superman capes off of our backs, kick-the-can and van rides across town with the other missionary kids to a school where I was only interested in getting good enough grades to not get a spanking.

Quick flits – trips to America. To the family by blood that I don't know. Being good at sports that Americans didn't play, and being bad at things that they did. Bicycling all over, learning to fish. Grateful when the time there was done and we were heading back home to Africa.

At 13, realising that I wanted to go to boarding school, that I was made for it, too independent. Rugby. Basketball. Soccer. The things that save a teenager from boredom while on an escarpment campus with a view unparalleled over the Rift Valley. Learning to compete. Learning friendship. Learning to question. Learning business through action, and through spoken day dreams of wannabe entrepreneurs.

It's generally good, all of it, a history I wouldn't trade. It's this uncommon past that allows me to travel, communicate and build so easily between worlds and cultures.

There is a strange mixture that formed my character. A combination of travel, mixed cultural experiences, tough education facilities, hard fought victories and losses, trainings for a foundation of belief in something bigger than myself. All this as I touch two worlds – the raw, gritty reality of my home country, mixed with the wealth and ease of my parent's country.

When I'm asked why I do the things that I do (as the co-founder of Ushahidi, iHub, BRCK, Savannah Fund, AfriLabs, Maker Faire Africa, and others) it has to be seen through this lens.

My parents were linguistic missionaries in Southern Sudan. Most people who grow up as children of missionaries don't go into business. I, however, had other ideas and from the age of eight I had turned over a wooden crate, cut a hole in it, and was selling gum on the mission station in Nairobi out of my mini-kiosk. I didn't think of it as much more than a way to get spending money, as that wasn't something that was in great supply in our family. I saved money too, for things like buying my first bicycle – as my parents didn't have the money and my dad thought it would help me appreciate the value of money. He was right.

The idea of making money was natural for me, and it was solidified when I was thrown together in boarding school with one of my Kenyan room-mates who was just as enthralled by it. We hatched and executed on plans for selling old clothes, buying food in town and reselling it at school, writing book reports for less voracious readers, among other enterprises even less glamorous and not always profitable.

*From 1980. Each morning started with my father taking my sister and me to Juba Model School in South Sudan. Photo courtesy of author.*

All this led to a discussion with my mother one day while I was home on holiday, where she told me that she was worried that all I would focus on was making money – that there were more important things than that in life. This conversation set a tone for my life, where I still followed my business instincts and path towards entrepreneurial activities, but refused to let money be the primary driver.

# Ushahidi and the 2008 Kenyan Election Crisis

I sat frustrated in front of my computer, holed up in a farmhouse in rural Georgia as news of the mounting tension and violence came out of Kenya. What a place to be, with limited Internet access while the country I call home was beginning to burn.

Being disconnected allowed me time to think, time to write, blog and read what others were thinking and doing as well. If technology allows us to overcome inefficiencies, isn't that what I was looking at? There was definitely a shortage of information, so could we use technology to do something about it?

Fortunately, Ory Okolloh, an old Kenyan blogging friend who was using her blog as a nexus point for journalists and others to get the word out, had an idea:

> *Google Earth supposedly shows in great detail where the damage is being done on the ground. It occurs to me that it will be useful to keep a record of this, if one is thinking long term. For the reconciliation process to occur at the local level, the truth of what happened will first have to come out. Guys looking to do something – any techies out there willing to do a mashup of where the violence and destruction is occurring using Google Maps?*

I Skyped with her about the idea, then sent an email out to the Kenyan technology community via the Skunkworks email (a local technology contacts list), and waited. Nothing. Not right away, at least. Maybe guys in Kenya were too busy and couldn't take the time to do anything at that moment. Instead, I called David Kobia, founder of one of Kenya's biggest and oldest online forums, Mashada. I had written a blog post about him and his organisation a few months previously, so perhaps he would be open to talking about the idea I was formulating.

Later I would become familiar with a few of David's habits. For example, he doesn't often answer his phone. Fortunately, on this occasion, I was able to catch him during a long drive to Atlanta. We talked for a few minutes about the idea of creating a platform for Kenyans to report what was going on around them, and to also aggregate the news that was coming out of the country.

David was hesitant. Before he could say 'no', I asked him not to make a decision, and instead promised to supply some mock-ups by the time he arrived in Atlanta so we could chat more the next day. Three hours later I shot off some early designs to him.

The very next day David sent me a link. He had created the first version of what would later become Ushahidi.

We hurriedly organised ourselves and set up a Skype chat with Ory, Juliana Rotich and Daudi Were, and started discussing what we should call this new thing. I remember our preference was for some easily pronounceable word, like 'kuona', which means 'to see' in Swahili. Someone else had already registered the website address for that, so we considered alternatives whose website addresses were still available. The word 'ushahidi', which means testimony or witness, was proposed. Could we get the .com? Yes, but non-Swahili speakers wouldn't be able to say or spell it. 'It doesn't matter. This will only ever be used in Kenya', one of us piped up. 'Buy it, we have other, bigger things to worry about'.

Two days later Ushahidi was launched to the world. The day after launch a friend donated an SMS short code allowing us to receive reports by text message. We now had a basic application allowing anyone to send a report in via email, mobile phone, or web form. It was rudimentary, but it worked.

The time line was rapid:

- January 3 – Idea (blog post)
- January 6 – Prototype built
- January 9 – Global launch

The most pressing issue for us was time. If we were to make any difference with the website we had to get it up 'now'. There was no room for 'it would be cool if' discussions – we could only consider the essentials. This was software product triage.

## TRUST

Let's take a step back. What enabled five seemingly loosely connected bloggers and techies to conceive, create and launch a new web app in just a few days?

There were two factors. First, all of us were part of the young and vibrant Kenyan blogosphere. Second, four of us had met at what would later turn out to be a seminal event on the continent: TED Africa in Arusha, Tanzania in the summer of 2007.

In short, we all knew each other already and had a feel for our personalities through our blogs. The TED event allowed us to actually meet and develop some mutual trust. When things got crazy, we knew that we could reach out to each other and rely on the others for support during a rough time.

Juliana Rotich was upcountry in Eldoret, a town in western Kenya. She gathered stories and helped verify what was coming in.

*The Ushahidi core team: Linda Kamau, Juliana Rotich, Erik Hersman and Brian Herbert. Photo courtesy of Ushahidi.*

Daudi Were was in the capital, Nairobi. As a founding member of the Kenyan blogosphere, he helped get other people involved. He also gathered stories and pictures, and helped verify reports with non-governmental organisations (NGOs).

Ory Okolloh was in Nairobi at the outset, but had returned to Johannesburg, South Africa by the time we launched Ushahidi. She used her blog to aggregate stories, pushed even more news and information to Ushahidi, and got others engaged.

David Kobia built the platform, creating new features and adjusting things as necessary, determined by what was happening on the day. His genius for simple solutions that worked ended up saving us.

My job in the beginning was to help David on the platform, but then quickly turned to managing media with Ory, building our supporter base and raising awareness.

We worked throughout the nights and at weekends. We took time out from our normal jobs and put aside client work in order to create, and then run, Ushahidi in Kenya. This went on for two months, into

February, until there was a peace agreement in Kenya. Throughout this time old friends like Ethan Zuckerman, and new friends like Patrick Meier, helped us overcome numerous hurdles along the way.

The mainstream media picked up on Ushahidi early, around January 12th, attracting considerable attention from the Kenyan diaspora. We quickly learned that many big crisis deployments were driven by the desire of those from the affected area to get information from family and friends. This would later be referred to in our lexicon as 'pothole theory', after we realised that 'people care about the pothole on their street, not the one two streets away'.

By this time, several important truths had come to light:

- The technology was nothing special. In fact, the Ushahidi platform could have been built four years earlier if someone had had a need for it.
- People wanted to tell their stories. They wanted others to know what was happening in the face of media intimidation, or about their inability to gain access to a particular area.
- We caused a stir by asking ordinary people what was going on. This bottom-up approach to information gathering during a crisis was either interesting or unsettling to the traditionally top-down humanitarian industry, media houses and government.
- Many of the NGOs that we asked to help verify incidents didn't want to share information or cooperate at all. Juliana later described this as 'data hugging disorder'. It put something of a chip on our shoulders about the ethos of NGOs, and raised questions internally about who they actually serve.

## USHAHIDI FOR THE REST OF THE WORLD?

It was not long before other people started asking us whether we could 'do Ushahidi' in their country. By March 2008 there was unrest in Chad, and xenophobic attacks had started to become a big issue in South Africa. We said 'no'. This wasn't our day job. If we spent even more time away from our other work we would not have been able to pay our own bills for much longer.

The Ushahidi site had been built in .NET, a software development environment that David knew, enabling us to set it up quickly. We told others in these countries that they could have the code, and gave it to them. The South Africans used it to set up UnitedForAfrica.co .za – I don't remember the Chadians doing anything with it.

We were surprised early on that we'd failed to find software that would work for our particular situation in Kenya, and that no one had

built any type of crowdsourcing software for a map 'mashup'. Ushahidi had taken us about three days to build. We realised that if we made the Ushahidi software freely available it would allow others to do in three hours what took us three days.

*Ushahidi in use during the 2011 Liberian elections. Photo courtesy of Ushahidi.*

None of us could take the time off from our normal lives to do this, or to do it properly anyway, so we set about seeing whether we could find funding that would allow us to create an organisation to manage it. By now it was April, and the five of us talked and put an ultimatum to each other – will you be a part of a new 'Ushahidi, Inc.' organisation and dedicate one year to it, if the money was found?

David, Juliana, Ory and myself agreed to form the organisation. Daudi decided to stick with his own web company in Kenya, although three years later he would rejoin Ushahidi.

A month later we won the NetSquared challenge, worth $25,000. This allowed David and I to put our consulting companies on hold and start redesigning, finding coders and rebuilding the Ushahidi platform as a free and open source software platform for the world to use. Challenges like NetSquared are important as they give new, young, unknown start-ups an opportunity to get recognised, and winning can give validation in the eyes of donors who hold the purse strings.

In August 2008, Humanity United gave us $200,000 which provided each of us with a salary and enabled everyone to work on Ushahidi full-time. As I think back to those first conversations with funders, I remember how strange it was dealing with grant funding, as all of us had been on the business side of the fence until then. There were a few tense calls where neither side could understand the other's language, but in the end we were able to find a common mission. We realised we wanted a platform that would allow others to organise themselves and make a difference in their part of the world, with a lot less effort than we had in Kenya.

I also remember how shocked I was when I was told that a platform for crisis situations shouldn't mix political crisis with other types. After all, they said, there was a big difference between political, environmental and other crises. This didn't compute for me, so I told them to think of Ushahidi as nothing more than what the Red Cross should be doing online.

This, of course, begged the question of why the Red Cross (or others) hadn't already built Ushahidi. To this day, I hypothesise that large organisations have a hard time innovating – there's just too much money and bureaucracy in the way – and that it's the smaller, faster, nimbler organisations that tend to do the most interesting new stuff.

## WHERE WE ARE NOW

The core Ushahidi platform has changed the way information flows in the world, and is today used in over 150 countries. It has been translated into 35 languages and has been deployed over 40,000 times. From earthquakes in Haiti and Japan, to floods in Pakistan, blizzards in the US, fires in Russia, and elections in East Africa and South America, it has been used by individuals, civil society groups and government. The top use cases are for crisis and disaster response, election monitoring and civil society coordination. Millions of people have benefitted from its use.

Ushahidi has also been widely used by funders to governments as a way to gather information about their work in an effort to improve decision making. Ushahidi's tools allow for easy data collection and analysis for feedback on anything from projects to opinions. Ushahidi hopes to continue to support decision makers in their use of these public tools to help gather public feedback about their projects, making their public consultation process more open and transparent. For example, the Government of Paraguay (in partnership with Fundacion

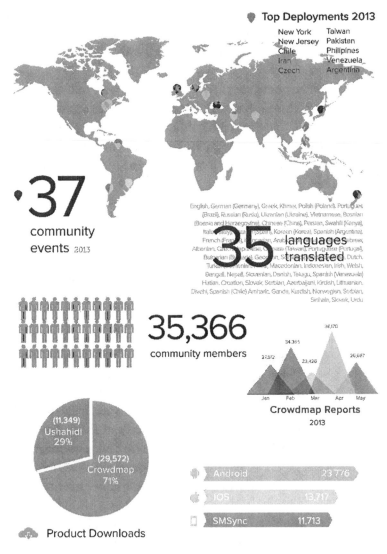

*Image courtesy of Ushahidi.*

Paraguay) have used Ushahidi to gather feedback and opinions for mapping poverty. They used it as a survey tool to gather feedback on government initiatives, poverty levels and needs, then used this to determine how they apply resources. Ushahidi hopes to support more innovative initiatives such as this.

## How I Think about Africa

When I look at the challenges we face in Africa, I see them from the perspective of an entrepreneur. Challenges are opportunities – and we are practically overrun by them.

By 2008 and the making of Ushahidi, I had been writing about the use of technology on the continent for a couple of years through my WhiteAfrican.com blog. I started to get to know other early bloggers and get connected to people who were as interested in how technology could help catapult the continent forward. This led to the creation of a website called AfriGadget, a place where we showcase stories of African ingenuity, and practical innovation in the face of problems. It's about the micro-entrepreneurs, the makers on the side of the road and the university inventors.

Through this writing I was connected to those who would later become my network for future endeavours. This is how I got to know Juliana, David, Daudi and Ory, who would become the founders of Ushahidi. This is how I started talking to Emeka Okafor who would invite me to TED Global in Arusha, and who would be my friend and co-organiser of Maker Faire Africa. This is where I met the early tech enthusiasts in Nairobi who would go on to create Skunkworks, the local techie email list serve – and from where the conversation at BarCamp 2008 would plant a seed that would grow to become the iHub.

In our read/write world of the web, publishing our thoughts and ideas is the single greatest way to build a foundation towards something that doesn't yet exist. It's a long road, it takes years, but with consistency and focus it opens doors that we don't even know are there.

I wrote about the Ushahidi idea before it was launched, getting the concept across for quicker adoption. I wrote about the iHub idea for over a year before it became reality, because no one wanted to fund it.

I wrote about the 'maker' culture in Africa for three years before we created an event around it, allowing interested parties to start congregating around the idea.

The opportunities that I've been a part of in Africa didn't come fast or easy. They took years to build and few were interested in paying for them at first. Some were a product of being in the right place at the right time, with the right people. Others were a product of a past track record and a network of people I knew who were able to open doors that wouldn't normally open.

A few things that I've learnt along the way:

*(1) Everything needs a champion, someone that inspires people to build towards what doesn't yet exist.*

If you get enough people to believe, then it becomes real. If you're not that person then the idea won't become reality. You need to really care about it. It's just as important for you to inspire your team as the wider community.

My job at Ushahidi is to frame and explain what we're doing – for myself, for the team, the media and for funders so that we can hit above our weight. So that we ourselves are inspired to challenge the status quo. So that others are inspired to join and support this movement, or start their own.

*(2) Traction is more important than anything else.*

If you can show a little progress then others come on board much faster, community grows more rapidly and people with money pay more attention. Sometimes you'll have to do this early kick-starting on your own, with your own money. Remember, you need to really care about it.

The BRCK is an Internet communications product designed and made to work in emerging markets. I had the idea to do this side project within Ushahidi about four months before I could get the other founders to agree to it. It took us another six months to get a prototype together. The truth is, it's a miracle the transport authorities allowed me on any flights with those early versions in my bag.

These early prototypes, products that were ugly and only vaguely worked but ones you could touch and feel, provided the early traction within Ushahidi that allowed us to keep going. Team members could pick a BRCK up and start imagining what it would be, which gave it enough legs to keep going as a product. We could show it to the board to get buy in. We were digging deep into our pockets to make it happen, but because there was something to see, something to show, it was 'real' and it was able to move ahead.

*(3) Those who push harder and longer, win.*

Life in Africa has a certain level of friction.

I spent a year looking for someone to fund the iHub idea. It turned out that no one wanted to put $200,000 into creating a space for the tech community in Nairobi. There was nothing like this and it sounded crazy, unnecessary. The Ushahidi founders knew there was something there though, so we figured out a way to get funding to allow it to happen through our own organisation.

In late 2009, a couple of early believers from the Kenyan technology community came together to form the advisory board. We started kitting out a space, technologists started coming, and we realised we had stepped into a much larger vacuum than we thought. We were overwhelmed by the technology community in Kenya's desire to connect. Suddenly, the technology companies we originally approached understood and started to seriously support the idea. It all looks great today, but it took years.

## RELUCTANT, OR ACCIDENTAL?

Honestly, I don't think we were reluctant innovators. We weren't thinking about being innovative. We weren't thinking about money, or what type of business we would create. We weren't thinking about anything other than solving a specific problem, quickly.

In the end, our focus was what made it work. We were building a tool that we needed. We were scratching our own itch. It was something where we were the users and we had the drive to build it at the same time.

# Our Lessons Learned, For Others

So many times I've seen people with a good idea do things in the wrong order. Here I highlight three of the biggest mistakes so others might avoid making them.

**They think of the money first.** If you do good things, money comes. I've never put it first on our list of things to think about. It comes somewhere after product discussions and user needs, but before personnel issues and travel. Yes, money is important for the long-term viability of your organisation and/or platform, but it's not the deciding factor for the first six months. If what you're doing cannot be done without money, on nights and weekends, then you don't care enough, or it isn't a big enough problem to solve.

**They don't have the technical person on their team to build the tool.** You should not outsource software development. It should be a core competency for any software-related organisation. If one of the co-founders isn't a strong coder, then find one before you do anything else.

**They become bogged down by organisational issues before they have a prototype.** You have nothing yet, so don't sweat the small stuff – such as organisation set-up – until you have something worth spending time on. I've seen a number of promising start-ups derailed by spats between their founders over equity, working titles and ownership issues. Go easy. If you can't trust your potential co-founders, the project is doomed anyway.

## Keeping Ahead of Ourselves

Since 2008 we've tried to keep a culture of innovation alive within Ushahidi, letting everyone make quick decisions and reducing bureaucracy in order to maintain agility. This has led to some other interesting products, including the iHub (Nairobi's innovation hub), SMSsync (a mobile app that sends incoming text messages over to a website), Crowdmap (a simpler, more rapid-deployment version of Ushahidi which we host), SwiftRiver (which analyses news and information streams and tries to make sense of them) and, more recently the BRCK (a device which helps people connect to the Internet in resource-constrained environments). Organisations have to fight to keep nimble and open to seemingly crazy new ideas, ones that are really different that allow change beyond the incremental.

## In Closing

It's helpful at this point to frame innovation – to think through why innovations happen at all, and which power structures lead to them being identified as innovative. After all, innovation is just a new way of doing things.

In any industry, society or business there's a status quo at play. These are generally legacy structures, set up for a time and place that needed that design. Think big media in broadcasting and print, and how it has been disrupted by the Internet, mobiles and social media in the last decade. How about government? How about the humanitarian sector? How about the energy industry?

All of these industries were seen as 'innovative' when they came into their own, decades and centuries ago. Now they are legacy in both infrastructure and design, and their relevance in their current state is in question. By their nature they fight to maintain the power structures that keep them in the position that they hold. Changes to the foundations on which they stand are not only scary, but deadly.

Innovation comes from the edges, so it is no surprise that innovators are found on the margins. They are the misfits among us, the ones who see and do things differently. They challenge the status quo and the power structures that prop this up, so are generally marginalised as a reflexive and defensive action.

Think about what you're really looking for when you say you want innovation in your sector. Because, when you do, what you're really asking for is the outliers, the disrupters and the rebels to have their way. You're asking for a new way of thinking and doing – and if you're in a position of power within an industry, you're going to likely find things a little uncomfortable.

When I think through what a reluctant innovator is, I think it's someone who is making change happen simply because the current

47

situation doesn't allow for them to act, to meet their goals, or fix the wider problem. Reluctant innovators tend to be disruptive, sometimes because of their own nature, but more often due to their unwilling- ness to believe that the current state is good enough. They ask ques- tions and don't automatically believe what they're told. Most seem to be thrust into it unwittingly at first, and it's only stubbornness and a certain level of naivety that keeps them going when most others would have quit.

At Ushahidi we clearly have this healthy mix of questioning and stubbornness, and certainly jump in at the deep end without looking too often. It's this penchant for creative independent thinking within, at every level, which allows us to keep trying new things – where we keep a culture of experimentation – and being okay with something not working right away, pivoting, and then trying again.

## ACKNOWLEDGEMENTS

The story of Ushahidi wouldn't have been possible without the vast community that deploys the software around the world, or the many individuals who give their time to make the platform better by fixing bugs, adding features and generally coding for a better future. Five years on, the core Ushahidi team still surprises me with its brilliance and commitment. Thank you for your efforts and sacrifices in what is ultimately a crazy work environment. Finally, to Juliana, David, Ory and Daudi, the journey has only just begun, and I couldn't have asked for better travel partners.

# 3

# DATA-POWERED DEVELOPMENT

## Joel Selanikio

*Parachuted into the middle of sub-Saharan Africa with a brief to collect public health data, and confronted with a laborious, environmentally wasteful paper-based system, paediatrician Joel Selanikio finds the perfect outlet for the skills he acquired as a Wall Street computer consultant.*

## AN ACCIDENTAL INNOVATOR

*'Name the greatest of all inventors. It is accident.' — Mark Twain*

When Ken Banks told me about this book, and the theme of 'reluctant innovators', I'll admit I didn't think it really applied to me. As someone trained in science, I've never been reluctant to look for new solutions when old approaches were failing.

Good science is always oriented towards innovation. When things don't work out in the lab, you brush off the dust and clean up the broken glass, adjust your theory, and come up with a new one.

I have had my share of luck, too. For example, the luck of choosing to do my paediatric residency right next door to the US Centers for Disease Control and Prevention (CDC). That put the right set of skills and concepts – public health and epidemiology, along with my computer background – in the path of the right problem: the lack of good health data. Definitely a lucky break for me.

Reluctant innovator? No. Much more accidental than reluctant.

## EARLY DAYS

When I left college in the late 1980s I had a degree in sociology but had also taken a course in computer science. I was lucky enough to get a job working as a computer consultant for Chase Manhattan Bank (now merged with JP Morgan), and I worked for that bank for a number of years, helping them figure out how to connect their mainframe-based databases with the 'personal computers' that were coming out at the time.

While the work paid well enough, at that young and idealistic age I was looking for a calling and not just a job, and I soon left Chase to pursue first my pre-med qualifications and then medical school. Medicine, it seemed to me, would challenge my intellect, was oriented towards serving others and, yes, would let me make a good living.

At that time I honestly thought that I was leaving behind my work with information technology – not realising that a tsunami of IT was just picking up speed and would be transforming the world, and that my skill and understanding of IT might be useful in such a world.

In fact, though I did not realise it at the time, my computer expertise would later become a major driver of my life's path, as IT grew enormously important in all of our lives.

*Lesson 1: quite often we are oblivious to the great societal and technological changes occurring around us.*

Medical training is famously long and arduous, and mine was no exception. I spent one year studying the pre-medical requirements I had never taken as an undergraduate, then four years at Brown University Medical School – not the best years of my life, but among the most interesting and challenging. This was followed by three more challenging and exhausting years of paediatric residency at Emory University.

During medical school I was able to earn money for room and board and books by doing computer programming on the side for my old colleagues at Chase, which was a huge financial help. It also kept me thinking about technology – though I still didn't think that would ever be applicable to a career in medicine!

When I was approaching my final year of paediatric residency, I was presented with a choice between two options: doing further 'sub-specialisation' within paediatrics (e.g. becoming a paediatric nephrologist, or paediatric oncologist), or going into private practice.

While those were usually framed as being the only two options available, I also learned of a third option: doing a fellowship at CDC.

I'm sure most paediatric residents never even know that this possibility exists, and I hardly understood what CDC was or did, but by luck I had done residency in Atlanta, just a mile or two from CDC, and there were many at Emory who had a current or past affiliation with it.

The CDC-connected people seemed to feel that I'd do well there. To this day, I'm not quite sure what they saw in me, or why they thought it was a match, but I was intrigued enough to apply to the Epidemic Intelligence Service (EIS), a CDC fellowship programme lasting two years, during which a fellow was expected to learn statistics, epidemiology, and – most importantly – the practical aspects of public health, from media relations to outbreak investigations.

Since the EIS was founded in 1951, partly due to US fears of Cold War bioterrorism, EIS officers have led all sorts of investigations into deaths and disease around the world.

If you've seen the movie *Contagion*, you will have a sense of what the EIS does: Kate Winslet plays an EIS officer investigating a raging epidemic that eventually kills her. Since that movie was years in the future, I had visions of exotic field epidemiology in my mind, rather than death from Ebola or other infection, when I was accepted into the programme.

Over the course of my EIS fellowship, and my subsequent years at CDC, I would investigate outbreaks in Chicago, Borneo and Haiti;

respond to hurricanes and anthrax attacks, help recover pieces of the doomed space shuttle Columbia from the Texas countryside; and work on malaria, measles and other infectious diseases still common in poorer countries.

It was this latter work, which typically involved collecting a lot of data, that first turned my thoughts to the possible application of information technology – and specifically the mobile technology that was just being born – to the needs of global health.

During this period of my life I thought that CDC was my career, full stop. Looking back, though, I realise that my time at Chase, at Emory and at CDC were just three preliminary stages helping me to add three skill sets – computers, medicine and epidemiology – that I would

*This grainy shot is the only photo I have from my early CDC days, taken while responding to a hurricane in the Virgin Islands. Photo courtesy of author.*

later combine into my real life's work at DataDyne: creating technology that solves problems for global health and international development.

## THE DATA PROBLEM

During all the various activities I was pulled into while at CDC, the single common thread was 'data', but not the kind of data to which I was accustomed while working as a paediatrician. CDC introduced me to the concepts of 'public health', and taught me that determining the cause of a disease in a whole population, or a group of people, involved a different set of skills and a different kind of thinking than determining the cause of disease in a single patient.

Clinical doctors are usually focused on the data from one patient at a time, and the way we present that data is typically as a chronology or 'patient history'. In my clinical practice at Georgetown University Hospital, I very rarely look at anything like a spreadsheet, and cannot ever remember performing any statistical analysis on any patient's data.

By contrast, public health focuses on populations rather than individual patients, and one of its most potent tools is the collection of large datasets (just picture a big spreadsheet). These kinds of data might be related to the percentage of people in the USA who are HIV positive, or the percentage of rural Bolivians who have access to clean water. They might quantify the percentage of children eligible to be vaccinated in Zambia who actually receive their vaccinations, or the percentage of pregnant women in Burma who die from infections.

Such data allows public health professionals to establish baselines, plan activities, measure progress (or the lack of it) and effectively pursue many other essential and lifesaving activities.

Without these datasets we are stuck with guessing and approximating and extrapolating, which are never as useful as actually knowing. And even incomplete data are much better than nothing. To quote computing pioneer Charles Babbage:

> *'Errors using inadequate data are much less than those using no data at all.'*

The problem is that in global health – and in global development in general – we are not usually choosing between 'good data' and 'better data'. We are usually faced with minimal data, old data, or no data.

*Lesson 2: We don't know what you think we know.*

I find that those not working in the field are often astonished to discover this. Those working in the field, on the other hand, are rarely surprised: they live and work in a 'data desert' throughout their careers.

Just a few examples of the things we just don't know (i.e. the data we don't have):

- How many refugees there are on the planet.
- How many clinics in poor countries are currently without lifesaving drugs.

- How many children were born last year in Bolivia or Bhutan.
- How many children died last year in Cambodia or Congo.

Amazingly, after years of spending billions of dollars collectively on HIV/AIDS in Africa (with, it should be noted, clear lifesaving effect), none of the organisations involved can tell us whether the prevalence of HIV/AIDS over much of the continent (i.e. the percentage of people in the population infected or showing symptoms) is going up or going down.

I've found that many people assume we know all these things. Surely our health institutions aren't spending millions, or billions, without really knowing the result? I assumed that, too, until I was dropped smack into the middle of sub-Saharan Africa to collect data and I began to realise the extent of the problem. A friend of mine likens my reaction to that of Neo in the film *The Matrix*, when Morpheus explains to him that his most basic assumptions about the world are incorrect. I thought I lived in a world run (or at least mostly run) by data, but I found out otherwise. And just as with Neo, after I realised this, the more I investigated, the worse I discovered the situation to be.

There are many reasons why we often lack even the most basic data, though the most frequently cited reason – lack of money – clearly does not apply to the HIV/AIDS in Africa issue I just mentioned.

Other reasons can include poor organisation of health departments, inertia, lack of supervision, lack of understanding of the importance of data, fear of change, war and other security issues.

And, of course, people and organisations (and donors) are often less than enthusiastic about collecting information that may show their activities in a bad light: as noted in a recent comment from a user of our Magpi software that is collecting data on education in sub-Saharan Africa:

> *'[The Ministry of Education] doesn't like data we collect, because it shows they are not doing their job.'*

It would be difficult or impossible, even for a large organisation or group, to deal with all of these issues. Given my background in computing plus medicine plus public health, I began to feel during my time at CDC that there was one problem that I might be uniquely suited to tackle: the unbelievably inefficient use of paper forms to collect required data.

## THE PAPER PROBLEM

This problem, which I thought my strange journey through banking and medical school and government might have put me in a good position to address, wasn't directly concerned with the issues mentioned above, but rather with the technology of paper forms that were (and still predominantly is) used to collect all the global health data.

Paper forms have dominated data collection in health for generations, both in clinical medicine and in public health. Think of all the forms used in a single clinic: the patient registry, the drug supply books, the blood supply records, the patient medical records, consent forms, staff records, lab reports, and many more.

In poor countries, where few people ever access a clinic, public health practitioners are responsible for the health of most, through clean water campaigns, vaccination campaigns, bed net distributions, and many other activities. And without collecting data in surveys and other activities it is simply not yet possible to know very much about the population. If you want to know whether someone smokes, you need to ask them. And if that someone happens to live in Sierra Leone, you have to go there to ask them.

Because of these factors, it is in public health, with its need for gathering and analysis of large datasets, that paper creates the greatest problems for health in poor countries (with all due respect for the current push for electronic medical records in the USA and elsewhere).

## PAPER IS *SLOW*

Imagine a single survey to be administered to 5,000 households in a poor country, with a couple of hundred questions on twenty sheets of paper. That amounts to 100,000 sheets of paper. In many such locations, it is likely to take several months, at least, to do the 'data entry': to type the data on those sheets of paper into a computer for analysis. Sometimes, it can take considerably longer – even years – before the data can ever be put to use in saving lives or improving health.

And, not uncommonly, the data are never actually entered into a computer at all. Think about that. All the weeks if not months of data collection, all the labour of the data collectors, all the money spent, all the benefit that could be derived from the collected data ... all comes to nothing.

With electronic data collection, of course, there was the possibility that all that time and effort of data entry could simply be eliminated.

## AN ENVIRONMENTAL DISASTER

Frequently, hundreds of thousands or even millions of sheets of office paper are used (then, typically, warehoused or just discarded) for just one field survey. And just one single survey of 5,000 households involving twenty sheets of paper per household is roughly the equivalent of twelve trees.

With thousands and thousands of these surveys, and other data collection activities, taking place each year – this represents hundreds of thousands of trees that would be saved if the data were collected instead on mobile phones or tablets (which are in many cases going to be produced for other purposes anyway).

Wasting trees is not the only way in which paper-based data collection is an environmental nightmare. Because it is heavy it increases fuel costs for all the vehicles that are used to carry it to the field. In the example of a 5,000 household survey, those 100,000 sheets of paper weigh about 1,100 pounds (500 kg) – and the EPA suggests that every additional hundred pounds in a vehicle reduces its fuel economy by 2%.

Finally, the production of every sheet of paper can use as little as 1.5 cups (0.35 litre) or as much as three gallons (11.3 litres) of water, meaning that our household survey consumes as 'little' as 10,000 gallons of water (about 38,000 litres) – or possibly as much as 300,000 gallons (more than 1 million litres).

So, just to review, our single 5,000 household survey consumes:

- Twelve trees
- Thousands of gallons of fuel
- Hundreds of thousands of gallons of water

And that is just for one single survey. Can you imagine how many trees, how much fuel, and how much water was consumed for the US census in 2010 – which was done on paper (despite the very large number of Americans that have access to the Internet)?

## A GLIMMER OF HOPE: THE PALM PDA

So while CDC was immersing me in the data process, and I was coming to realise just how little data we actually had, a device invented to help businesspeople keep track of their calendars – the Palm PDA – gave me a little hope that progress could be made.

The Palm PDA, originally called the Palm 'Pilot', was the first really affordable hand-held computer. It debuted in 1996 at a price of just $249 (the ill-fated Apple Newton, released a few years before, had cost almost three times as much), and it had more than enough computing power to display forms, given the right software.

For me, that software came in the form of a program called Pendragon Forms. Pendragon was the first software I knew of that allowed me to easily design mobile electronic forms. I took to it quickly, and began experimenting with using it for field data collection in poor countries.

In 1998, I worked with a group of US Army nutritionists to do a nutrition survey of Burmese refugees in a Thai refugee camp. The resulting publication, *Mobile Computing in the Humanitarian Assistance Setting: An Introduction and Some First Steps*, published in 2002, was the first to detail the use of mobile electronic data collection within international health, or within the humanitarian setting.

It was my hope at the time that our demonstration of the use of new Palm technology for humanitarian public health purposes would open the floodgates. Surely everyone would want to use this new technology now that we had told them about it?

But that's not what happened.

## The Floodgates Didn't Open

In fact, what was most remarkable in the wake of our publication was the widespread failure to use Pendragon, or any other software, to collect data with Palm or other PDAs. It wasn't that no one was using this – or similar – technology, but I doubt that at the height of the PDA era even 1% of public health data was being collected this way.

In trying to make sense of this, I managed to grasp at least one reason: it was too hard. I just stated that Pendragon 'allowed me to easily design mobile electronic forms', and it was true. For a long time I thought of Pendragon as being easy.

At a certain point, however, I realised that what was easy for me, with my computer science and programming background, was not easy for most people. Optimal use of Pendragon required some programming skills – skills that the vast majority of people simply do not have.

Imagine designing a coffee maker that required a computer programmer to set up each morning. Could you see yourself using it – unless you were a computer programmer?

*Lesson 3: Technical people always underestimate the scarcity, and the cost, of their own expertise.*

This concept made me believe that the key to increasing adoption of technology like Palm PDAs for data collection was to make it so easy that the average health worker could use it – without having to hire any technical experts.

## EpiSurveyor Phase 1: It's the Technology

While I was working with Palms and Pendragon at CDC, my future business partner Rose Donna was doing similar work at the American Red Cross (ARC). ARC was involved in what would become one of the most successful global vaccination campaigns in history, the Measles Initiative. A critical success factor would turn out to be the pioneering use of mobile technologies for the collection of data that let them understand when they were doing well and meeting programme goals, and when they were not.

I met Rose in 2002, while temporarily assigned to ARC, and with both of us tiring of the bureaucracy in large organisations we decided we would try to work together in the hope of moving further and faster, and with fewer meetings.

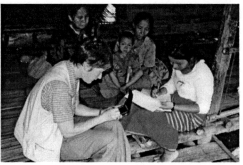

*Collecting data in Thailand with Palms, circa 1998. Photo by author.*

In retrospect, I realise that meeting Rose was one of the most important points of my life, because:

*Lesson 4: You cannot do this alone.*

We were lucky enough to secure a few grants in relatively short order, from the World Bank and the ARC; enough to hire a programmer (my computer skills were definitely too rusty by then). We quickly began creating what I named 'EpiSurveyor': the first do-it-yourself system for mobile electronic data collection that didn't require any technical expertise at all (the name was changed in 2013 to Magpi).

EpiSurveyor consisted of a PC-based program that allowed the user to design forms, and a Palm PDA-based program (what we would now call an 'app') to deploy the forms in the field.

Initial use of the software was promising, but revealed that it still was just not easy enough, and there were two issues in particular that proved difficult to overcome.

## EASY TO USE, HARD TO INSTALL

As we developed a prototype, and then a first real version, of EpiSurveyor, Rose and I began to fly around the world to train programmes that might want to use it. This was more than a little ironic, since the software was designed to be do-it-yourself.

A major problem was that the initial version of EpiSurveyor followed the model of all software at that time: the PC component had to be downloaded and installed onto a laptop or desktop, and many people had difficulty with the process. Furthermore, it required that the Palm Desktop software provided with the PDAs also needed to be installed, and that the Java utility software also needed to be installed.

This presented a series of hurdles that tripped up many people trying the software, and we needed to engineer around this problem. Unfortunately, I didn't initially know how we might do this.

## No PDAs in Africa

The second major problem, in addition to installation, that we encountered in those early days was that Palm PDAs were essentially a rich world product: it was difficult and/or expensive to buy them in African countries, where we initially focused. This led to years of wheeling rugged Pelican cases full of PDAs from country to country.

The lack of a locally available technology for data collection was an enormous hurdle, and we wasted time trying to find ways to, quite literally, get enough grant money to buy a Palm PDA for every African health worker. Like everyone else, we would never in a million years have imagined a local market for pocket computers in Africa or other parts of the developing world (and, boy, were we wrong!).

*Lesson 5: It is easier to move electrons than molecules: it's much easier to build and scale software worldwide than hardware.*

## Miracle #1: Hotmail

As I was wrestling with all the difficulties our EpiSurveyor users encountered in installing our software, I happened to notice that all the health workers I was working with in sub-Saharan Africa had a Hotmail account.

At first I didn't think much about this, but after a while I began to see the parallels between what we were trying to do (unsuccessfully) and what the Hotmail people were doing (very, very successfully). We were both trying to distribute software to everyone who needed it.

But all the approaches to distributing technology that I had learned within government involved flying around the world to every country. And lots of conferences, and lots of training sessions – and, by no means coincidentally, a lot of per diem payments, a lot of frequent flier miles, and a lot of contracts for trainers and consultants.

I should know: I was one of those trainer/consultants.

But Hotmail wasn't doing it like that at all. Hotmail was getting software capacity out there but not flying around the world to do it. Hotmail wasn't training people, Hotmail wasn't paying for per diem, or hotels, or airfare.

Of course, Hotmail was just the beginning. I soon saw my African colleagues using LinkedIn and Flickr and Gmail and Google Maps, and of course none of those things required any training. Or programmers. Or consultants.

*Lesson 6: Technology creates new business models; new business models drive technology.*

This dramatic difference in approach, I realised, wasn't driven by technology but by business model. Hotmail had used every tool at its disposal to drive costs down. First, it used the web and shared 'cloud' servers to decrease hardware costs. Then, it simplified the software so that no training or support was required.

With costs close to zero per user, Hotmail was able to support itself not through training and consulting and flying out to locations where Hotmail was used. Instead, it could more than recover costs just through advertising revenues.

And with its free, simple email program available to anyone with a browser, Hotmail spread rapidly to even the poorest regions on earth (not, yet, to the shepherd in the field, but definitely to the professionals at their desks in the capital cities).

I wasn't so much interested in supporting EpiSurveyor by advertisements, but I was very interested in worldwide scale. I realised that if we could move EpiSurveyor to the web it would mean that no one would need to install it anymore (you don't install web apps, you just type their web address into a browser), and just as importantly no one would need to hire a consultant or trainer to use it anymore (not even me). It might even be possible that we could have people using EpiSurveyor in every country on Earth.

So in 2009, EpiSurveyor became the first web application created for international development.

## MIRACLE #2: THE MOBILE PHONE

The web certainly made it easier for us to move software around the world, but that didn't solve our issue with hardware. We still needed a cheap mobile computer on which to run the app.

This problem has famously been solved by the tidal wave of mobile phone adoption through rich and poor countries alike (see the figure on the facing page), and the difficulties of exporting devices to poor countries is borne by the mobile manufacturers and distributors – not by the global health community.

This meant that we could piggy-back on the success of mobile, and that's what we did. As we moved EpiSurveyor from the PC to the web, we simultaneously moved the mobile component from the PDA to Nokia's Symbian 'feature phone' platform.

Almost immediately afterwards the Palm company began a rapid collapse, to our shock. Had we not made the lucky move to phones, EpiSurveyor would have died with the Palm. But as it turned out, the Symbian platform would soon be under siege, as the iPhone and Android phones began grabbing market share – so we soon added iPhone and Android versions of our mobile app.

*Lesson 7: Never rely on a single hardware platform.*

## EPISURVEYOR PHASE 2: RAPID GROWTH

My initial hunch that we needed to follow the technology model of Hotmail (and Facebook and Flickr) was really borne out by our experience. During the period of June 2009 to December 2012 we saw EpiSurveyor

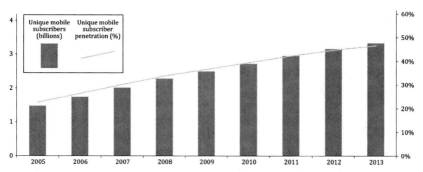

GSMA Intelligence defines total unique mobile subscribers as unique users who have subscribed to mobile services at the end of the period, excluding machine-to-machine. Subscribers differ from connections because a unique user can have multiple connections.

*Unique global mobile subscribers.*
*Graph courtesy of GSMA Intelligence.*

users online rise from zero to more than 10,000. And just as predicted from the Hotmail model, those users were active in more than 170 countries – and we had never even spoken with the vast majority of them.

That was a slightly bitter pill to swallow. I had always enjoyed going out to the field, travelling in exotic places, and providing training. I missed it, and still do. But we had learned an enormously important lesson.

*Lesson 8: If your technology requires an expert on the ground every time it's used, it will never scale.*

It turned out that our enjoyable training trips to the field were in themselves an enormous obstacle to widespread use, and eliminating them increased our user base dramatically. 'Self-service' was definitely the way to go.

## Not Just for Epidemiology Surveys!

Though we had initially created EpiSurveyor for epidemiological surveys, when we changed our distribution channel to the web we quickly found that users were discovering the software and using it to collect data on a whole variety of things. This is probably the most amazing

63

part of what we do and how we do it. Almost every month I learn about some other user or organisation that has discovered Magpi (the new name for EpiSurveyor since January 2013) and has put it to use doing something I never imagined.

A few examples follow below.

## CAMFED

Camfed is a UK-based charity that promotes the education of girls. With programmes in five sub-Saharan African countries, Camfed pays families to keep girls in school, and monitors school activity for the girls in its programmes.

Its old monitoring system, on paper, required a year or two before the data would even reach some kind of report.

Now Camfed uses Magpi and has real-time monitoring of its programmes. Data is collected on basic phones by teachers, then uploaded to Magpi, then sent to Salesforce.com for analysis and web dashboards. All in all, an amazing use of technology – and the whole tech implementation has running costs of less than $15,000 per year for all five countries combined.

*Photo courtesy of JSI.*

## JOHN SNOW INC. (JSI)

JSI is a US-based organisation working in global development that has used Magpi extensively. It has also provided funding for us to add additional features that have benefited all of our users.

JSI has pioneered the use of Magpi for supply chain management – one more thing we never intended it for – utilising it to efficiently gather and analyse stock availability and case management data for malaria medicines at health facilities each quarter in Tanzania, Ghana, Liberia and Zambia.

From JSI's website:

> *'EpiSurveyor [Magpi] has replaced paper-based data collection and, by automating data entry analysis, has improved the speed and accuracy of completing and disseminating quarterly reports... The information gathered through mobile phones provides quick, actionable information to PMI, USAID, MOHs, and in-country partners regarding stockouts, supervision and training problems, expiring drugs, and more. It enables decision makers to intervene sooner to resolve potential problems.'*

## KENYA MINISTRY OF PUBLIC HEALTH AND SANITATION (MOH)

Kenya MOH has been a long-time partner as we developed EpiSurveyor/Magpi, and was the first place we tested the software back in the PDA days, and the first place we tested the software using phones. Now there are many experienced Magpi users at MOH, and they use it for everything from one-off surveys to tracking polio outbreaks, to monitoring the twice-yearly Malezi Bora (Child Health) week in collaboration with UNICEF.

Many, many others are using Magpi as well. Physicians for Human Rights is using Magpi to document sexual violence in Congo and elsewhere. Abt Associates uses it to monitor tuberculosis treatment. Researchers in South America have used it for studies of the human papillomavirus. And the Canadian government used Magpi to monitor outbreaks of disease on commercial pig farms.

The message from all this, of course, is that the world population is much more clever and resourceful than any organisation or individual could be. By making Magpi simple and free for almost all users, we allow anyone – regardless of how much money or how many connections they have, or whether we even know they exist – to gain from the benefits of mobile data collection.

*Kenya MOH fighting polio with Magpi. Photo by author.*

## EpiSurveyor Phase 3: It's the Business Model, Stupid!

Our move to the cloud did not just allow more users to sign up – it also gave us visibility into who was logging into the software. We could see, in real time, which people from which organisations were logged in at any one time – and who was not. This led to some uncomfortable revelations.

## My Career as a Professional PowerPointer

In going over our user activity logs for the online EpiSurveyor app, I quickly realised that no one from any of our funding organisations was listed. Apparently no one who was paying us had ever seen our working software!

This didn't seem to make sense. Who would pay for software without ever looking at it? And if our funders hadn't seen the software, what information were they using when they decided whether to fund us each year?

Slowly, and uncomfortably, I realised that my idea of myself as primarily a technologist was wrong. I was not being paid to create great technology – after all, none of our funders had any idea at all whether our technology was good or bad.

I was a storyteller. I was being paid to produce stories about technology saving lives in poor countries. Stories that I sold once a year to our funders, in the form of PowerPoint presentations. Stories that they then distributed to their constituents.

*Lesson 9: Your job is what people pay you to do. This is sometimes different from what you believe your job to be.*

I can't emphasise it enough. I am confident that even if we had produced no software at all my excellent PowerPoint skills could have kept the money coming. And in my experience, this is all too common in international development. Good communications skills can make bad technology, or even non-existent technology, smell like a rose – and building a good slide deck is cheaper and faster than building good technology.

Keep in mind: I'm not saying that people with great technology should not tell that story. I'm saying that in many cases I see stories about technology substituted for the sustained and scaled development of really useful software.

*Lesson 10: Organisations in international development have learned that it is easier and cheaper to tell stories about sustainable and scaled technology than it is to create it – and just as effective for obtaining funding.*

For me, the burning question became 'how do we get evaluated primarily on our technological skill, rather than on our PowerPoint skills?' In other words, how do we become real technologists, not just storytellers about technology.

And for that, we decided to throw ourselves at the mercy of the market.

## THE FREEMIUM IS THE MESSAGE

During the PowerPoint era, our product was stories, and our customers were grant-making foundations. Looking once again to Silicon Valley for inspiration, I identified a new business model for EpiSurveyor that I thought fitted perfectly to international development: 'freemium'. In 2010, after having been the first web-based application for international development, EpiSurveyor also became the first freemium application.

Freemium ('free' + 'premium') is familiar to most people from their use of Skype. Most people know that there is a free version of Skype that is used to make computer-to-computer calls, and there is also a paid version of Skype that is used to make computer-to-phone calls.

Because Skype uses the Internet to transmit its call data efficiently, its costs per call are exceptionally low, and close to zero for computer-to-computer calls. This cost-efficiency allows Skype to 'give away' computer-to-computer calls, and still make enough revenue with computer-to-phone calls to be profitable.

Even today, after Skype was acquired by Microsoft and pushed to increase the percentage of paying users, about 75% of users never pay anything.

I thought this kind of model would be great for international development because in my experience a small percentage of organisations had huge amounts of money for technology, but the large majority had almost no money for technology.

So the small percentage of organisations with money could be our customers, buying our technology product. We'd still tell stories, of course, but that wouldn't be our primary job anymore. Those organisations would be paying us for our software – and if our software wasn't good enough, they wouldn't pay us.

As with Skype, free users get a great deal, but so do paying users. In almost every instance, the cost of paying for our software is a tiny fraction of the cost of collecting data with paper, and cheaper than other electronic systems that require technology consultants and programmers.

Most importantly, freemium allows us to break down the relationship between the size of an organisation's budget and the kind of technology it can use. In international development, generally organisations get the technology they can afford. Rich organisations – or organisations that can successfully attract the attention of a rich donor – can afford to build or buy great tech. Other organisations get little or nothing.

But just as Gmail is available to everyone, no matter how much money they make, Magpi is available to every organisation, from the smallest local project to the biggest multinational activities. And the projects with big budgets that buy Magpi subscriptions end up supporting its free use for all those other organisations.

That is deeply, deeply satisfying to all of us at DataDyne.

## THE ROAD GOES EVER ON

Since moving to the cloud, and switching to a freemium business model, there have been a lot of other changes. We changed the name of the software from EpiSurveyor to Magpi, as our users began showing us that it was useful for a lot more than epidemiological surveys.

We originally had two price tiers (free and 'Pro' for US$5,000 annually), but later expanded to include a US$10,000 annual 'Enterprise' subscription for larger organisations.

In autumn 2013 we added 'Magpi Messaging', super-easy, super-affordable and super-fast basic messaging capabilities that will let every organisation create an SMS-based education system, or recorded-audio vaccination reminder system, in minutes. Or just use SMS to keep their field staff organised.

I suspect that Magpi Messaging will prove even more popular than Magpi data collection because there are many more people out there looking to communicate than to collect data.

I don't know what comes after Magpi Messaging, but I think that at DataDyne we'll keep doing what we've been doing:

- identify a technology like mobile data collection that is useful but barely used because it's too complicated and expensive;
- make it simple and affordable by using the cloud and mobile and freemium; and
- sit back and watch all the crazy, cool and lifesaving things people do with it.

# 4

# DIAL M FOR MEDICINE

## Josh Nesbit

*Intending to ground himself in the realities of global health
during his internship in rural Malawi, Josh Nesbit discovers that
it is hard to sit on the sidelines and soon finds himself proposing
a mobile technology solution to overcome the difficulty of
connecting patients, community health workers and hospitals.*

I wanted to be a doctor. Or, at least, that was what I told anyone who asked. It did seem like a good idea. I could work tenaciously towards a set goal, earning a position that would allow me to care for people. Despite my young, unsettled mind, it was hard to imagine a moral philosophy at odds with healing.

I was an undergraduate at Stanford University at the time, studying Human Biology with a concentration in Global Health and Bioethics. When it came time to choose a location for an internship, there was only one real option – St Gabriel's Hospital in rural Malawi. My younger

71

sister and mother had built a relationship with hospital staff the previous summer, we were connected to a foundation supporting the palliative care programme, and the hospital was ready to put me to work. A substantial – and reasonable – fear as an adventuring twenty-something was that I would be in the way, more of a distraction than a helper or change agent. I arrived in Malawi knowing I could at least count pills in the dispensary. Each pill in each packet of drugs was hand-placed.

The main goal, I told myself, was to ground myself in the realities of global health. I learned quickly that it was hard to sit on the sidelines. I met patients walking or oxcarting over one hundred miles to reach the hospital, accompanied by worried family members – their guardians responsible for food, water and bathing during the patient's hospital stay.

The outpatient ward hallway was always packed full of people – the single doctor attending to patients was overwhelmed. Over 500 community health volunteers were doing the best they could to take care of people in their own communities, but they were just as disconnected from the hospital as the patients.

The first health volunteer I met was Dickson Mtanga. He would travel 35 miles to the hospital at least once a week, accompanying patients on journeys or coming along to deliver messages. He carried a notebook, tightly wrapped in newspaper. I soon learned he was keeping meticulous, hand-written patient notes during his home visits for the treatment supervisors at the hospital. Dickson was supporting people in his community being treated for HIV/AIDS and tuberculosis (TB). He washed their bed sheets, monitored any side effects, and bicycled or walked to the hospital to provide updates to clinical staff. He served as his community's only connection to the hospital.

One day I visited Dickson's home. He was a proud grandfather, and his extended family provided a warm welcome. After greetings, I pulled out my mobile phone and checked for signal. To my amazement, I had fantastic coverage. This was it! I might have a helpful idea. With the thought still very fresh, I sat down with Dickson to discuss: What if he used a cell phone to stay in touch with the hospital and coordinate healthcare for his community? What if we used this brand new cellular infrastructure, which had sprung up less than a year beforehand? It was a simple idea, an approachable challenge, and a shared vision from the start.

The following journal entries recount the earliest days of Medic Mobile's first project in rural Malawi, beginning in the summer of 2008. I stumbled into opportunities and introductions – securing a small grant from the Haas Center for Public Service, meeting Ken Banks when he was developing the text messaging tool FrontlineSMS (a two-way text messaging platform designed primarily to work for grassroots non-profits in resource-constrained settings). I may have been slowly turning already, but my life's steering wheel was about to be yanked towards a new path.

## 20 June 2008: Maps and Meetings

I'm very happy with how things have started off. Almost immediately upon arriving, I pitched the communications programme idea at the hospital management meeting. Most of those in attendance I knew from my previous stay in Namitete, and they seem happy to have me back.

I've discovered that props are useful. So, I lugged my suitcase into the conference room, revealing about 100 cell phones. I also flopped around the approximately 100,000 units of air time credit that I had purchased at the airport. After a quick demonstration of FrontlineSMS, ideas started flowing – and not just in one direction. I'm finding that ideas developed in the USA regarding the programme's potential usefulness (e.g. patient follow-up, TB and HIV drug adherence monitoring, fielding the community's medical questions, etc.) are really resonating here.

After a bit of drudge work (putting in SIM cards, adding credit to the phones, recording numbers, testing FrontlineSMS, etc.), we are ready to start the pilot.

I am calling the chairs and vice-chairs of both the Community AIDS Committees (CACs, or 'cacks') and the Village AIDS Committees (VACs, or 'vacks') for a meeting on Monday morning. It's set for 8am – I'm hoping they'll trickle in by 10am. This first group of Community Health Workers (CHWs) will be the pilot within the pilot. After monitoring their activities for a week or so, we'll look to expand to another group – as the matron says, we'll start with those who are 'hardest working.'

I spent the day in Lilongwe, trying to find decent maps of the area that the CHWs hail from and work in. First, I tried the District Health Office. No maps, but the doctor coordinating health information for Lilongwe was very interested in the communications initiative – specifically, the possibility of scaling up to cover the entire Lilongwe district. In an attempt to stay ambitious but grounded, I left her my e-mail and other contact information.

Next, I headed to the Department of Surveys. Like the government hospitals, the state buildings are treacherous. Quite literally, I had to guess which alleyway to wander down – I was finally consoled by a piece of paper, duck-taped to a door, which read, 'Digital Mapping.' I put in an order for TA Kalolo and TA Mavwere (don't ask me what 'TA' means, because I have no idea), and was told to come back in a few hours. After a few 'fees' were processed, I had my maps.

## 23 JUNE 2008: 'WHEN CAN WE START MESSAGING?'

I have to believe that today's events were endowed with the elements of a promising beginning. The first phones are in the field! Before I get too ahead of myself, let me explain what's put me in such an optimistic mood.

We called the chairs and vice-chairs of the volunteer committees (Community AIDS Committee, Village AIDS Committee, and the 'People Living With HIV and AIDS' (PLWHA) support group) for a meeting at 9am. They came in together, some on bikes, most on foot. Considering that some travelled over fifty miles (that's definitely an underestimate), this was quite the event.

I had been up since 6am testing phones and FrontlineSMS, and I was eagerly awaiting the group – equipped with Cokes, Fantas, lemon cookies and a broad smile.

We met in the old Nutrition Rehabilitation Unit, which had been stocked with assorted chairs. After everyone sat down, the hospital's matron greeted the group. After making sure each of the CHWs could understand slow English, she opened the meeting:

*'I know that times are difficult, but we must make improvements step by step. Do babies just start to run? No, they start just sitting. Then, when they see something beautiful, they wiggle their stomachs and arms, trying to reach for it. Soon, they can crawl, then they start walking. We can take steps forward, together. This is a pilot – we are learning new vocabulary today, too! You are the first to do this. It is not enough to try. We must do it.'*

After that poetic introduction, the matron told them they'd be receiving cell phones. This news was greeted, almost immediately, with cheers and applause.

The matron handed over the ecstatic audience to Alex and me, and we explained how to operate the phones (Alex is a male nurse, who works within the Home-Based Care programme). I had every single ounce of the audience's attention, as I started, 'First, just open your phone!'

We had an outstanding time teaching the CHWs how to use the phones. It started with group chants of, 'Messages! Compose Message! New Short Message!' The majority of the CHWs hadn't texted before, so we spent some time teaching them. By the end of the session, each of the health workers could flawlessly type 'St Gabriel's Hospital,' apostrophe-and-all.

After a few hours of rigorous concentration and seemingly inexhaustible patience, we took a break for snacks. During break, we discussed logistics.

The CHWs all claimed to have access to electricity. It seems that most will have to pay 10 Kwacha (a few cents) to use the nearest electricity hub. When it's necessary, they (or someone from their village) will travel to the hospital to recharge the phone, free of fees. This isn't altogether rare, as the CHWs often accompany patients to the hospital.

After the matron and Alex explained baseline expectations for communication, the CHWs took over the meeting. Pascalia and Verona, the two Community AIDS Committee chairs, were especially emphatic. Pascalia stood, declaring, 'The hospital does what it can to help the volunteers. We must do what we can to work hard. Remember, just because we are the ones who came to the hospital today does not mean the hospital loves us more than the others.' Verona responded, looking straight at me and pumping her fists, 'I will work much harder!'

The frequency and type of communication the CHWs will maintain with the hospital will depend on which programme the CHW is enrolled in. For example, those involved in TB drug adherence monitoring will alert the hospital when a patient is deviating from a regimen. Similar expectations were agreed upon for the ARV (antiretroviral drugs) monitors. Home-Based Care volunteers will be messaged when a patient needs to be traced or if a follow-up is needed. Those involved in organising peer support groups will use the system to co-ordinate meeting times and locations. With any luck, and plenty of commitment, there will be a working network of CHWs, with St Gabriel's Hospital as a co-ordinating agent.

Before leaving, the group sent a sample text to the hospital's number (basically a mobile SIM card sitting inside a device which attached to the computer we were using), and we showed each CHW their respective message as it popped up in FrontlineSMS. It was an animated scene, for sure. I recorded some of their information (name, number, village, and respective programme), checked their starting units, and let them loose on the catchment area.

Needless to say, I'm looking forward to tomorrow, and the possibility of the first messages trickling in. With a smile on her face, Verona asked me, 'So, when can we start messaging?' A few of the CHWs joined me in responding, 'Now!' As they started home, I could see they were exchanging phone numbers.

## 24 June 2008: The Inaugural Texts

From Zakeyo Kaphanthengo: 'Ineyo ndinayenda mapesent awiri sakupeza bwino amenewa ndiavuto lakhasa.'

I thought I'd post it in Chichewa, to document its original form, but it translates roughly to: 'There are two patients, very sick with cancer.' Tomorrow Alex will take the hospital motorbike to Chilembwe, about 60 km away, to check on the patients. A quick text let Zakeyo know to expect him.

From Baxter Lupiya: 'Natenga ma ARV omwe anasiya aMwinama, omwe amamwalira dzulo. Ndibweletsa la chisanu. Zikomo.' Translated: 'I have collected the ARVs left by a patient who has died, and I will return them to the hospital on Friday. Thank you.'

From Benedict Mgabe: 'Mai laulentina adamwalira pa sabata kwa chamoto omweanali pa pa h.b.c.' In English: 'Laulentina, a patient in the Home Based Care programme, died on Saturday.' Terrible news, by any measure, but it saves the hospital a day-long trip to Chamoto to give Benedict more morphine.

I can't help but envision each of the hospital's CHWs with a phone in their hand, the hospital's number saved as cherished contact.

## 28 JUNE 2008: READY FOR MORE

We're ready to expand a bit. We heard from every one of the CHWs in our pilot group (some many times). In just a few days, we saw some tangible results. Here's one example.

Verona Kapagawani, who lives in TA Mavwere, alerted the hospital that a patient had run out of his meds.

A nurse at the hospital, familiar with the patient, responded that he should fill his prescription (he has chronic congestive heart failure) as soon as possible.

Verona responded, noting that she counselled the patient. He wasn't feeling well enough to travel, so she came to the hospital to pick up his drugs.

While chatting with the nurse, Verona charged her cell phone.

I ran into another CHW, Benedict Mgabe, at the hospital today. He's the chairman of the Community AIDS Committee, and he's texted me every day. With a smile on his face, he shook my hand and said, 'This is a very good programme! It is really helping us a lot.' Those two short sentences confirmed that I needed to have longer conversations with the CHWs, to gather their reactions.

We are using the pilot group to contact the next wave of CHWs, another ten volunteers, to be trained and given phones on Monday morning.

On the next page you'll see Alex (a nurse, who does most of the Home-Based Care community work) and Grace (who coordinates the ART (antiretroviral therapy) programme) using FrontlineSMS to text the group.

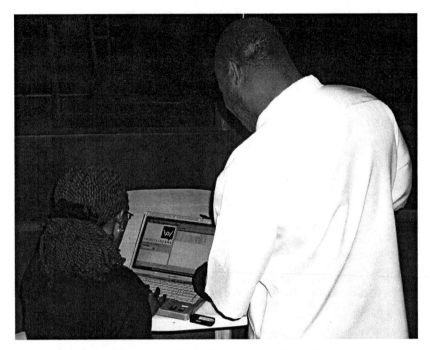

*The FrontlineSMS system in action at St Gabriel's. Photo by author.*

I had a long discussion with Dr Mbeya, the medical director at St Gabriel's, about making very definitive links between the hospital and the CHWs' activities. As the project grows over the coming weeks, we will create guidelines for reporting and follow-up, based on the specific programme. For example, the hospital has a lively prevention of mother-to-child transmission (PMTCT) programme, aimed at reducing vertical transmission of HIV. We'll develop a protocol for utilising the CHW network to follow up on mothers who have missed their appointments, and the CHWs will provide a link to the communities' pregnant population.

## 3 JULY 2008: INCREASED COVERAGE

This week, another group of jubilant CHWs were trained in texting. The week has gone very well, and the project's initial success has been noticed by each arm of the hospital. I took a minibus into Lilongwe, which turned out to be a fruitful venture – I rode into Namitete on a bike taxi wielding extra maps, an assortment of drawing pins, and a few surge protectors (which will establish a permanent location for CHWs to charge their phones at the hospital).

Each CHW who we train and provide with a phone will be placed on a map of the hospital's catchment area, using a colour-coded pin, depending on their programme (Home Based Care, ART Monitors, Reproductive Health Volunteers, Counselling, or Youth Volunteers). Particularly committed volunteers assume multiple roles in their community – they are distinguished by blue pins. The idea is to have the maps, with hundreds of CHWs' locations marked, displayed clearly for the clinical staff at the hospital. This way, a clinician looking to track down a patient need only consult the map, find the nearest, appropriate CHW's identifying number (written on the pin), and send out a text.

Tomorrow afternoon I'm attending the staff meeting for those involved with the hospital's ART programme. I'll be explaining the project, and the group will determine a protocol for communicating with adherence monitors in the field.

## 8 JULY 2008: A DIESEL-FUELLED RESPONSE

Today, Alex and I headed into the field. The goal was to find seven patients – the hospital had been alerted of their declining health by SMS, through seven different CHWs. The motorbike-enabled text-message-guided journey through the catchment area completed a (once) theoretical cycle: the CHWs surveying communities, then communicating their most urgent needs; the hospital gathering resources (diesel, drugs and medical advice), then travelling to the villages.

Often, we stopped by the CHW's home. After taking a picture, she ran home, put on her St Gabriel's Hospital 'Positive Living' shirt, and joined us for the consult.

A brief overview of some of the cases follows.

- An HIV-positive man, on ARVs, with Karposi's sarcoma and wet beriberi.
- A 13-year-old girl with stomach cancer and massive ascites. Pascalia is the closest CHW, but her bicycle 'ambulance' is not operable. So we texted Moreen, who is just a few villages away. She'll bring her ambulance, and take the girl to the hospital.

- A 72-year-old man, who is sputum-positive for TB, and was complaining of severe joint pains.
- A man, suffering from epilepsy, fell into a fire two weeks ago. He has developed a massive ulcer on his left heel. Below, Alex is explaining how to wrap gauze. The man was happy to let us take a picture of the scene.

*Alex treats a patient on one of his rounds. Photo by author.*

We met with the hospital staff when we returned – after traveling 100 km in six hours, and visiting seven different villages. Everyone agreed that the day was a success.

The entire hospital staff is now fully aware of the project and its goals. We are all moving in the same direction. The consensus is that a second, simple cycle, once disseminated, will greatly aid follow-up and monitoring programmes: the medical staff (looking to follow up on a TB patient, for example) consulting the CHW map, and contacting the nearest CHW; the CHW checking on the patient, and responding to the hospital with their status.

Tomorrow, we train another 15 CHWs.

## 14 JULY 2008: NEW IDEAS

Over the last week there has been a cascade of communication. A few examples, among many:

A man missed his appointment with a TB officer. A CHW was texted, who reported that the man had gone to Zambia for a funeral. The hospital will be notified upon his return.

An HIV support group met, and decided on new member guidelines. Via SMS, the group leader asked the hospital to print copies for the lot.

A CHW asked about ferrous sulphate dosages, so that he could administer the proper amount to an anaemic child.

Text messages cost 10 cents. Units can be sent from one phone to another via Celtel's Me2U service, but managing the units of 100+ phones manually is almost impossible. So I had to find a way both to monitor each phone's unit level and top up (replenish depleted reserves) automatically.

Before leaving Stanford, I engraved each phone's faceplate with a two-digit ID number. Using FrontlineSMS's auto-forward function, I have set up a system to automatically top up CHWs. When they are running low on units, CHWs can text '(ID number) Units' to FrontlineSMS. Subsequently, a message is sent to Celtel, with instructions to top up that particular CHW. System abuse is unlikely and avoidable – the volunteers know that FrontlineSMS records every message received, sandwiched by unit requests.

We are starting to explore additional functionalities of FrontlineSMS. Each CHW is given a kit of basic medications – a proportion of the questions that we are fielding involve those drugs. We will set up an auto-reply system so that any message containing a given drug name returns a summary – function, dosages, etc. – for that drug.

## 27 JULY 2008: CAUGHT SMOKING

A baker's dozen left St Gabriel's Hospital on Thursday with cell phones, trained and ready to communicate. On the next page, a CHW practices texting 'Malawi'. He is the Home-Based Care provider in his village, and runs an orphan care centre.

Text messages are notorious for being concise, hence the Short Message Service (SMS) protocol and its 160 character/message cap. Most of the messages to and from the hospital are brief, and to the point. Some CHWs, however, send stories – sometimes five messages in length. A few examples (translated from Chichewa):

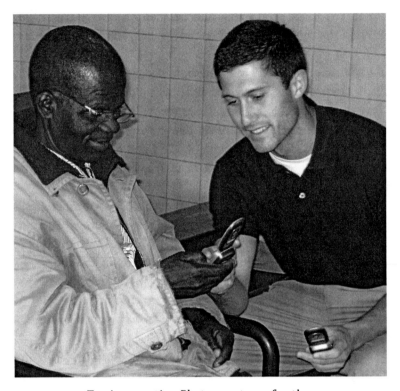

*Texting practice. Photo courtesy of author.*

*XX is refusing to use the condoms in his family, which has made his wife to be pregnant of three months and he also drinks alcohol much, and also likes women. In so doing I advised him not to stop using condoms and also to stop drinking because they are putting his life in danger. And his wife should start going to her doctor visits, like at St Gabriel's.*

*I found XX smoking, and he is on TB medication. He failed his first treatment in 2006, and this is his second treatment. XX is on TB treatment. He is taking the drugs following instructions. He is improving. XX had swollen thighs but she is improving. She is taking drugs following instructions – the guardian is strict.*

Both of these CHWs texted for the first time a little over a week ago.

I'm planning to video-interview a few of the CHWs this Tuesday and Wednesday.

## 4 AUGUST 2008: NEED-STRESSING COUCHED IN GRATEFULNESS

These days, the majority of the patient visits made by the mobile team are responses to SMS requests for immediate medical attention. Still, certain visits are scheduled follow-ups after patients have been discharged. Travelling with Alex, I realised that, at least half the time, the patient is nowhere to be found. Alex now sends a few quick messages to the CHWs overseeing the patients whom he is planning to visit, letting them know he will be stopping by. While he is out in the field, any response from the CHWs is forwarded by FrontlineSMS to his cell phone. This ensures that he sees patients who are available – and avoids 40-mile journeys to discover a patient is away, selling maize in Mozambique.

This past Saturday, we gathered the first 30 CHWs for a refresher course – explaining the automatic unit top-ups and the drug keywords (we've already had BB Paint, TEO, Panadol, and Multivitamin info requests).

I'm leaving Malawi this coming Friday, and heading back to Stanford. The general attitude of the CHWs might be described as grateful, yet realistic about the pressing needs of their families and friends – hence, the title of this post. Malawians are said to spend roughly 10% of their waking hours at funerals. The statistic does reflect troubling times – but it also demonstrates the blurred boundaries between family and fellowship. Villages are full of brothers, sisters, and mothers – some share heredity, but all share circumstances. Every text message sent by the CHWs has invited me to appreciate the true meaning and function of community.

## 14 AUGUST 2008: BACK IN THE USA

After a few days of travelling I'm back at Stanford. It was difficult to leave Namitete, but there is plenty to be done in the USA.

# 22 August 2008: Verona Kapagawani; Community AIDS Committee Chair

We interviewed one of the Community Health Workers involved with the pilot in Malawi. Verona spoke about why she started volunteering, how the SMS programme has changed her ability to care for patients, and what it means to be a healthcare volunteer. Here are a few of the messages sent to the hospital by Verona, in the first weeks of the pilot:

AK has a problem of CCF; his medicine is finished, and he is getting a bit better.

AJ is on TB treatment, he is taking the drugs following instructions. He is improving. AM had swollen thighs but she is improving. She is taking drugs following instructions – the guardian is strict.

Adherence: TN is alright. He is taking the drugs following the instructions. He did not miss any day.

PT is very fine, working hard in the garden. He did not miss any day.

# 4 December 2008: CNN – 'Texting to Save Lives'

That is the headline the CNN Technology site is using to pull visitors to a story covering the project. It is amazing to see Alex and Grace on the site, and I think Steve wrote a wonderful article.

# 20 December 2008: Back on the (Wet) Ground

I'm back in my old room at the hospital's guest house, and it's pouring with rain. I arrived just in time for the last Home-Based Care course – 21 new volunteer CHWs were reviewing referral procedures, patient rights, the contents of their drug kits, etc.

The photos on the facing page show a group copying acronyms into notebooks (top photo) and what they are writing (below right).

At the end of the session, the CHWs were asked to hand in a piece of paper describing the location of their home. Most of their responses were paragraphs long – some included extensive maps.

*Home-Based Care course attendees. Photo by author.*

Joanna, who is running PointCare's CD4-count outreach pro-gramme, relayed an inter-esting conversation with one of the CHWs a week ago. She travelled to their farthest site – a good 100 mile drive – and ran into Zakeyo, who said, 'You know, Josh is com-ing on the 19th.' I checked FrontlineSMS, and Alex had not warned him. It is exciting to know that the next time I see him, I will pass on a solar panel accompanied by a so-lar-powered light.

Tomorrow, I'm going to spend some quality time with FrontlineSMS – working through the communication over the last four months.

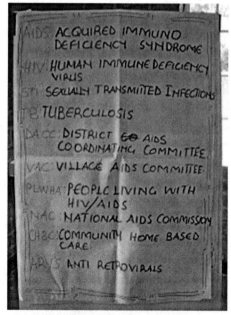

*Course notes. Photo by author.*

I have just two weeks before I return to Stanford, and I'm trying to make the most of it!

# 22 December 2008: The Real Story

Here's the truth – this project involves people, rich in character and experience. It's not only about the technology. If I'm interested in the technology fulfilling its potential, I have to pay attention to the people.

Case in point:

I spent yesterday mulling over text messages sent through FrontlineSMS over the last four months, noting which CHWs had communicated least. I put together a list of a few CHWs who I suspected might be having signal issues. Looking at the map, three of six CHWs on this list were clumped together – clearly, they do not have good reception.

I told Alex about my findings this morning. He took a look at the names and said, 'Well, Bernadeta took her phone with her to Zambia, we've discovered that Chrissy is not able to write her own name, and Jereman's phone battery was stolen while it was charging at the local barber shop.' My time away from the hospital almost made me forget the multitude of stories swirling around these phones and the hospital they are linked to. With 100 phones in the field, three random problems are to be expected.

Whether or not everyone agrees, I think personal stories convey a project's successes, as well as its failures. Silia, a hospital attendant who runs the hospital's TB programme, said yesterday, 'The SMS project is very, very good – I can get much more work done, instead of driving the motorbike everywhere. It's very simple – we can expect feedback about patients immediately.' I met the new hospital administrator today, and his second sentence was, 'You know, it's not only beneficial for communication. The volunteers are now committed to their work, and more will follow.'

I'm letting stories from patients, CHWs and the medical staff at St Gabriel's drive my exploration into this project's value. I turned to people for the direction of the initiative, and I'm turning back to them to measure part of its impact.

The first batch of solar panels arrives tomorrow.

# 25 December 2008: Tuberculosis, Meet FrontlineSMS

On Christmas morning, Silia stopped by the guest house to talk about the SMS programme. He is responsible for testing, drug provision and follow-ups for TB patients. He described how he is using FrontlineSMS and the network of cell phone-wielding CHWs. Almost all of what follows developed in my absence.

Some sputum-positive patients don't turn up to receive their medication. It is Silia's job to track down these patients and get them back on their drug regimens. Before the SMS programme, he was visiting an average of seventeen patients per week – this took him three trips on his motorbike. Each trip would take around nine hours. That's 27 hours per week spent tracking patients in various villages.

The SMS network has allowed Silia to share his workload with the CHWs. He now tracks an average of 20 patients per week via SMS. He simply texts the CHW nearest to a patient who has not turned up. As Silia says, the CHWs provide 'immediate feedback.'

The programme has been running for roughly 26 weeks. With the shift to SMS-based patient tracking, Silia had an additional 700 hours to utilise. Not surprisingly, he has been using FrontlineSMS to supplement other areas of his work.

He now visits an average of four patients per week, for different reasons. Some messages from the CHWs tell of patients who are too ill to travel to the hospital. Silia will respond by bringing a new supply of drugs. Other messages relay symptoms of community members, such as: 'A man has a chronic cough, and we suspect TB.' Silia will visit the patients, and collect a sputum sample. He will return to the hospital to do testing and send the results, by SMS, back to the CHW.

Finally, when patients at the hospital test positive for TB, they are told which CHWs near their home have cell phones.

Some numbers from the TB programme for the last six months: 700 hours of follow-up time saved, 450 follow-ups via SMS, (at least) $2,000 in motorbike fuel saved, 100 new patients enrolled in TB treatment programme.

# 27 December 2008: SMS for Patient Care, In Its Truest Form

I sat down with Alex today, to discuss FrontlineSMS and its impact on the Home-Based Care (HBC) programme at St Gabriel's. Essentially, he is a one-man, mobile care unit – focusing on chronically ill patients and those who simply cannot travel to the hospital. The backpack, pictured here, is full of medical supplies.

The SMS network has brought Alex to the homes of 130 patients who would otherwise not have received care. That amounts to about five responses, per week, to requests for remote medical attention.

*Alex with bike and hospital supplies. Photo by author.*

Before the SMS programme Alex was visiting around 30 patients a week, rotating through the HBC roster. He now follows up on five patients per week, usually checking in on those who have been recently discharged from the hospital. The CHWs take care of the rest – since the programme started, approximately 520 HBC patient updates have reached the hospital via SMS.

The difference in Alex's HBC activities amounts to about 500 hours and over $1,000 in fuel saved. He has responded to around 40 requests for healthcare supplies (usually dressing materials for wounds and cervical cancer patients). With FrontlineSMS blasting automated responses to drug inquiries and Alex responding to questions regarding basic care, the central SMS hub truly serves the CHWs and their patients.

Alex, who is a highly capable nurse, also holds full shifts in the male ward at the hospital, and is one of two staff members co-ordinating antiretroviral treatment for the catchment area. Given his multitude of responsibilities, any time saved in managing the Home-Based Care programme is extremely valuable.

The first batch of solar panels from G24 Innovations arrived today – I tested one of the products and it quickly charged my phone, to completion, during a thunderstorm. More on this later – we are gearing up for training and distribution on Monday.

## 29 December 2008: Full Charge!

This morning, we distributed the first batch of solar panels from G24 Innovations. I was also able to reconnect with CHWs whom I had not seen for a while. Of course, Alex ran the session.

To close the meeting, the CHWs sang a song for me that they had prepared – I'm not sure what the lyrics were, but 'phones' and 'messages' were included! Afterwards, I travelled with Dickson Mtanga and Mary Kamakoko to their villages – it took a good two hours on a bicycle. We spent another three hours biking around and seeing patients, before I started back to the hospital.

## 3 January 2009: Antiretroviral Texting

Grace Kamera runs the HIV treatment programme at St Gabriel's. She oversees antiretroviral therapy (ART) for the catchment area – which includes 250,000 people and an HIV prevalence rate of 15%. While there are a few government-run health centres in the area, St Gabriel's Hospital is the only facility offering HIV tests, and the only place to get treatment.

Many of the CHWs are ART monitors – they are trained to check on HIV patients, to see whether they are complying with the treatment regimen. Non-compliance undermines the treatment's efficacy and contributes to drug resistance. Given a limited number of choices for drugs, patient adherence is critical.

Before FrontlineSMS and the accompanying cell phones arrived, Grace was receiving 25 paper reports per month from the ART monitors. With 21 ART monitors equipped with cell phones and trained in text messaging, she has received 400 adherence updates since the outset of the project (15 per week).

If the paper trail had continued, each report would have been hand-delivered by a CHW. The average round trip is about six hours, so the SMS programme has saved ART monitors 900 hours of travel time.

If Grace receives an SMS regarding a patient's missteps, she will counsel them when they return for more drugs. The patients are well aware that the CHWs have cell phones, and they are grateful for the connection to the hospital (and Grace). Of all the patients who enrol in the ART programme, 80% agree to be monitored. The remainder fear stigmatisation within their communities.

Some patients do not turn up to receive their HIV medication. Grace says this is rare – 'They usually come a day or two late' – but it happens. She has used the SMS network to track 25 patients who have failed to show, asking the nearest CHWs to report on their status. Sometimes they have left, other times they are unable to travel or have passed away.

The hospital and the people it serves cannot afford a lack of connectivity. With Grace at the reins, ART monitors will continue serving their communities, 160 characters at a time.

## 11 JANUARY 2009: WHAT'S EVERYONE TEXTING ABOUT?

A couple of very committed individuals – my mother and sister – set out to answer that question. For four months, they translated every message from Chichewa to English.

My sister, Elizabeth Nesbit, decided to code and organise every SMS sent by the CHWs. As I write this, she is a sophomore at Rice University, making her way to medical school. She categorised messages by keywords and/or phrases (e.g. symptoms, supplies, patient updates/

referrals, deaths, requests for help, requests for visits, meeting coordination).

## 21 January 2009: Going Global

A lot has happened in the last six months. Everyone involved with Mobiles in Malawi (my early name for the project) is excited by the SMS programme's impact on healthcare delivery at St Gabriel's Hospital. The medical staff and participating CHWs have taken ownership of the initiative, and what is left of a public service grant will keep the programme running for 10–15 years – at just $500 per year.

St Gabriel's is certainly not alone in the challenges it faces as a rural healthcare provider. After witnessing the effects of simple ideas and equally uncomplicated technology on medical care, one thing was clear – each day that a clinic goes without tools that it wants and needs is a day with undue hardship.

Now I am talking with healthcare organisations working in 11 countries (Burundi, Malawi, Uganda, Zambia, Mozambique, India, Kenya, Ghana, South Africa, Peru and Haiti) about partnerships to expand the tools and strategies used at St Gabriel's to their respective sites. Details regarding these organisations and my role in supporting them will be covered on my jopsa.org website in the coming weeks. In addition to healthcare providers, I'm honoured to be collaborating with kiwanja.net, The kiwanja Foundation, the FrontlineSMS team and MobilizeMRS.

After speaking with global health organisations and the clinics to which they are linked, it is clear that 2009 must be a year of action.

## What Happened Next?

Over the next three-and-a-half years, the project grew from FrontlineSMS:Medic into a non-profit technology company, Medic Mobile, and work expanded to 20 countries across Africa, Asia and Latin America. By 2013, Medic Mobile's programmes supported frontline health workers, families and patients in 10,000 underserved communities, improving healthcare delivery for more than six million people. Tangible results continued, with stock monitoring across Malawi speeding up 134 times, childhood vaccinations in India jumping from 60% to 90%, and infectious disease surveillance halting outbreaks. Not bad for a project which cost a few thousand dollars to get going.

It has been an incredibly rewarding personal journey, too. Grit and an optimistic disposition have been trusted tools, helping me handle the sucker-punch-to-the-soul lows and appreciate the soaring highs. Personal values and the guidance of a small, trusted community continue to disrupt any and all five-year plans.

# 5

# WHERE THERE IS NO LIGHT

## Laura Stachel

*After watching local doctors and midwives struggle to treat critically ill pregnant women in near-total darkness on a Nigerian maternity ward, where an untimely power cut can mean the difference between life and death, obstetrician Laura Stachel delivers a solar-based solution that greatly enhances their survival prospects.*

*The woman had been in labour for hours and was suffering extreme pain. Her condition was deemed critical by the Nigerian medical staff and the decision was made to operate. The power grid was down. A nurse lit a kerosene lamp in the maternity ward. It barely lit the ward and was certainly inadequate for the operating theatre. We waited in the maternity ward, with the patient sitting in a wheelchair. The power surged back on, and we wheeled the patient to the surgical ward. A portable surgical lamp provided weak illumination in the operating room, adequate only by African standards. Using my flashlight, nurses prepped the patient for surgery. At the foot of the operating table, a*

*nurse held my flashlight and directed a beam of light towards the pa-
tient. This aided considerably, particularly during the subsequent two
power outages that occurred mid-procedure.*
— *Research notes, Nigeria, 2008*

In my obstetrical practice in the United States, I loved being a part
of the birth process – and considered it a privilege to be included in
the intimacy of childbirth. It was my duty to support and empower the
women I cared for. During labour, I often imagined an ancestral line of
women who had given birth, each bearing the next generation, leading
to this moment in time.

It wasn't until I spent time in the darkened maternity unit of a Nigerian hospital that I began to struggle deeply with the complexity
of what is medically known as maternal mortality – women dying in
childbirth. For most pregnant women, the idea is an anachronism. But
in the developing world, particularly in sub-Saharan Africa, death from
'complications of childbirth' happens hundreds of times a day.

As an obstetrician, I am trained to solve problems in pregnancy
and labour. I analyse what I see and chart a course of action. But the
problems I confronted on my first trip to Africa – the erratic electricity,
surgical delays because of poor lighting and lack of mobile communication, the scarcity of medical instruments, the inadequate staffing
and limited training– were symptoms of a systemic failure. Maternal
care was in dire straits for reasons far beyond any medical techniques
I could offer: poverty, lack of infrastructure, gender inequity, illiteracy
and politics all conspired against the health and survival of pregnant
women. Within the hospital, lack of reliable electricity stood out as a
major obstacle to providing effective maternal care.

I never expected to be a social innovator in the developing world,
let alone an advocate for solar energy for maternal health care. But
as I witnessed women struggling to survive childbirth in Nigeria, and
health workers trying their best to provide care in darkened maternity
wards, I knew I couldn't turn my back on this problem.

My first passion in life was music and dance. At the age of 17, I
entered Oberlin Conservatory and College to study for a career as a
concert pianist and modern dancer. I devoted myself to practice, spending eight hours a day in the music conservatory and dance studio.

In my sophomore year, my doctor discovered an irregularity with my ovaries. Without surgery, he couldn't discern whether this was cancerous or not. As I was wheeled into the operating room for diagnostic surgery, my doctor informed me, 'If it is cancer, you'll wake up with a big bandage and all your reproductive organs will have been removed. If it is benign, you'll only have a small bandage.'

In the recovery room, I reached for my abdomen before opening my eyes. A small bandage. I hadn't lost my ovaries. But the surgery had identified an ovulatory disorder that prompted a lot of questions. So many, in fact, that my gynaecologist quipped, 'If you have so many questions, why don't you become a doctor!'

It was a thought that had never occurred to me, but the idea resonated. Medicine would allow me to blend traits from my father (a scientist) and my mother (a clinical social worker). In my junior year, I left the familiarity of music and dance studios and enrolled in my first science classes. Medicine was a far cry from piano and dance, but the discipline I had developed in my artistic pursuits proved to be helpful in my classes. I studied alongside pre-med students who understood formulas and concepts that were absolutely foreign to me. It was a struggle, but I persisted.

My interest in medicine and healthcare deepened. I took an active role in women's health issues on the Oberlin campus. I became a volunteer peer counsellor at the college 'Sexual Information Center,' co-taught a course on the 'History and Politics of Women's Health Care,' organised campus-wide health education events, and worked with the Oberlin College Health Plan Board to expand student access to reproductive health services. These initial activities in health policy and education were immensely formative. An idea took shape in my mind: to become a physician who would have the power to make changes within the health care system.

After finishing up my pre-med requirements in the summer following college graduation, I spent a year in a research lab at the University of Chicago. I applied to medical schools all over the United States and was thrilled to be accepted at the University of California, San Francisco. As I moved through clinical rotations with my classmates, I found myself drawn to psychiatry – why people behave the way they do – and women's reproductive health, especially obstetrics. I also loved surgery, and believe that my years as a pianist endowed me with a manual dexterity that was an asset in the operating room.

At San Francisco General Hospital I had the privilege of conducting deliveries under the tutelage of seasoned midwives, and learned about natural childbirth, as well as the complications that could threaten the health of mother and baby. I was honoured to witness and participate in the miracle of childbirth. When it came time to select a specialty, I chose obstetrics and gynaecology, which allowed me to be part of the birth process, as well as to practise surgery. The field also satisfied my desire to connect deeply with my patients at such an important and vulnerable time in their lives.

I stayed at the University of California, San Francisco for my obstetric residency – four years of a non-stop training that occupied up to 130 hours each week. At the time it was believed that arduous working hours, including thirty-six-hour shifts, were necessary to prepare young obstetricians to handle any situation. The hours were intended to expose us to a wide range of complicated cases. As an intern, I remember being so tired on one occasion that I tried to decline my supervisor's request to assist with a Caesarean section. I was told that if I refused, I would be denied future opportunities to gain valuable experience in surgical skills.

My first full-time job was at a progressive holistic women's practice in Oakland, California, where I worked in tandem with midwives and nurse practitioners. From the start of my clinical practice I subscribed to the midwifery model – pregnancy as a state of health – rather than the traditional Western medical model – pregnancy as a time of risk, fraught with peril. This outlook would make it all the more jarring, years later, when I encountered women dying from complications of pregnancy and birth that I knew need not be fatal events.

As my career unfolded I had three children of my own, gaining firsthand experience of pregnancy and motherhood. It was quite a juggling act. My children recognised that their mother could be abruptly summoned out of the house to attend to a woman in labour. Family time together was often interrupted by an emergency call prompting me to bolt out of the door. My practice was extremely busy, and the thousands of patients who identified me as their doctor knew that there could be a six-week wait for a routine appointment. I gained a reputation as a caring physician who loved to talk with her patients and include family members in the process of birth, often encouraging them to help with the delivery. In my practice, complications of pregnancy were unusual and tragic outcomes were rare. Joy and happiness infused my work every day.

In 2002 I was plagued by persistent back pain that eventually radiated to my neck and arms, sometimes delivering an electric-shock sensation to my hands. During one particularly arduous delivery, a searing pain tore down my back, and I knew something was very wrong. An MRI revealed the cause – severe degenerating disc disease in my cervical spine, compressing the nerves to my right arm. I was told I had to stop doing deliveries, and later, to stop my practice altogether.

My hectic life as a physician came to a halt. No more piles of charts with messages needing my attention, emergency rooms calling for consultations, phone calls in the dark of night alerting me to impending deliveries. I was the patient, and my job was to get better.

I found a physical therapist, a masseuse, and an acupuncturist. I spent hours each day lying on my back, using neck traction and doing gentle exercises in an attempt to strengthen the muscles supporting my neck. I couldn't get through the day without pain, but learned to modify my activities to minimise the stress. I used a special anti-gravity chair at home, and learned to do many activities in the reclining position. I couldn't sit up for long, and my family came to expect to see me lying down during dinner and car rides. I did make some modest improvement, but a neurosurgeon told me I couldn't return to my work until I could go for a month without pain. That month never came.

A year after I had taken leave from my practice it became obvious that I needed a vocation that would be less physically stressful. What I initially viewed as a devastating setback, I now consider the beginning of the most fulfilling chapter of my life.

I had a long-held interest in population health, and enrolled in the School of Public Health at University of California, Berkeley. Sitting up for classes wasn't easy, but I loved being a student again, and was excited to be introduced to new fields of study. Through weekly physical therapy my physical endurance improved. Four years later, when an opportunity came to consult on a maternal health research project, I jumped at the chance. At that time, half a million women died each year in childbirth, 99% of them in developing countries.

The project fascinated me. In collaboration with Ahmadu Bello University Teaching Hospital (ABUTH) in northern Nigeria, UC Berkeley investigators sought to prepare local doctors to conduct research in maternal health. This was an issue of urgent importance, given Nigeria's high maternal mortality ratios. At the time of the study, Nigeria accounted for 2% of the world's population and 11% of the world's maternal deaths.

I obtained a research fellowship from the Bixby Center for Population, Health and Sustainability. Daniel Perlman, a medical anthropologist from UC Berkeley, was spearheading the Nigerian research efforts, and he shared with me the 'verbal autopsies' conducted by local research fellows – interviews with family members about the sequence of events leading to maternal death. Reading these transcripts introduced me to the depth of the challenges facing these pregnant women in need of emergency care. The obstacles they listed are known as the 'three delays', an extremely helpful framework for understanding the high rates of maternal mortality.

The first delay begins at home. Impoverished, far from a medical facility, and typically without decision-making authority, rural women are often reluctant to ask for help until labour is seriously compromised. Culturally, the male head of the household is the one who will make the decision to seek medical care, a move that is likely to involve spending a significant sum of money on clinic fees and transportation costs. Much time is lost as the family weighs these factors.

Transportation is the second delay, as more time is lost trying to find public transportation, a car, or a motorcycle to transport the woman. It was the third delay, though, that troubled me the most.

According to the field notes from Nigeria, many women who sought medical care for severe complications of labour were turned away from health facilities – as many as four or five health centres – in their quest to get care. Some of those who were finally admitted to an appropriate facility were so critically ill that little could be done to save them. But the reports suggested that sometimes the health facilities failed to provide timely care.

Daniel Perlman was looking to conduct research inside the hospitals to understand more about hospital delays. Being an obstetrician in public health school made me uniquely qualified to help. I was invited to meet with the Nigerian team and conduct participant observation at a Nigerian hospital.

In March 2008, I boarded a plane to Abuja, Nigeria. It was my first time in West Africa and I was eager to utilise my obstetric knowledge in some way. I knew little about what to expect. As an anthropologist, Daniel suggested I keep an open mind and avoid excessive literature research in advance of my visit. My job was to observe obstetric care, and to report on what I learned.

We drove from Abuja to Zaria, a predominantly Muslim city in the Nigerian state of Kaduna. Daniel introduced me to the principal members of the research team – the Population Reproductive Health Partnership – obstetricians and family health physicians who were committed to improving maternal health research and outcomes. Soon he planted me in Kofan Gayan State Hospital, a large state hospital on the border of Zaria's 'Old City.'

Inside the metal gates I took note of the layout of hospital. Each medical ward had its own building. Most of the divisions – maternity, gynaecology, male medical and surgical, female medical and surgical, and paediatric – were familiar to me as an American doctor. What wasn't familiar was the 'VVF' ward, occupied by women suffering from vesico-vaginal fistula – one of the worst obstetric consequences of prolonged obstructed labour. VVF is a permanent fistula, or hole, between the bladder and vagina, resulting in permanent leakage of urine. In my time at the hospital, I learned that women in this ward waited weeks for a specialist surgeon to arrive to repair the defect, then more weeks to heal from surgery. Because the fistula, and the resulting urine leakage, had caused many of the women to be shunned by their communities, they utilised their tenure in the hospital to learn new skills, such as sewing.

For my research, I was drawn to the maternity ward – a one-storey building containing the labour and delivery room, the maternity room, and the eclampsia room. The maternity room had twelve metal patient beds in two rows and a nurses' station at the other. Newborn babies shared their beds with the mothers. I learned that 150 deliveries occurred in this hospital each month, with significant loss of life.

I was immediately struck by the grim conditions. The labour room had four bare metal delivery tables, a limited collection of obstetric instruments, a newborn incubator that hadn't worked in years, a broken lamp, two newborn scales in poor condition, and little else. There were no mattresses, sheets, bright lights or monitors characteristic of an American hospital. Most striking were the frequent power outages that left the hospital in darkness, creating an immense barrier to care.

*Maternity ward in Nigeria with a nurse working
in near-darkness. Photo by author.*

I learned that electricity was rationed in Nigeria, that the public utility grid in Kaduna operated only a portion of each day – at most, twelve hours. When the hospital had power, it could use its lights, refrigerator, surgical suction and other energy-dependent devices. When the power was down, the hospital was incapacitated. A diesel-fuel generator tried to compensate during evening hours, but fuel was expensive, and the generator was used sparingly.

I had not predicted the challenges facing my Nigerian colleagues. At night, I observed maternity care, watching helplessly as doctors and midwives struggled to treat critically ill pregnant women in near-total darkness. The dim glow of kerosene lanterns often provided the only illumination. Without electricity, doctors had to postpone Caesarean sections and other life-saving procedures. When the maternity ward was in darkness, midwives were unable to provide emergency care and, on occasion, would turn patients away from the labour room door, despite their critical need for care.

The most upsetting example of this was when a woman in labour was brought to the hospital late at night, bleeding heavily. She had a critically low blood pressure. The presumed diagnosis was uterine rupture – a life-threatening condition requiring immediate surgery. The hospital was in darkness, unable to conduct surgery or provide the immediate blood transfusion necessary to save the woman's life. The midwife advised the family to go elsewhere to get care, and the family was sent back into the darkness. It was hard to imagine she would survive.

One night, I witnessed an emergency that set me on the path to where I am today. The labour room was in near darkness, and I settled at the foot of the bed of a seriously ill pregnant woman with eclampsia. Brought to the hospital unconscious, she had suffered several seizures at home in labour, according to the family members who hovered at her bedside. Although she had been given a single dose of anti-seizure medication at the hospital, the woman had another convulsion; her family attempted to hold her body down. When the seizure was over, she lay still, her breathing abated, and I thought she had died. Tears welled in my eyes.

Anyone would have found this woman's suffering disturbing, but as an obstetrician, I found it intolerable. Eclampsia, although serious, was an eminently treatable complication of pregnancy. I stood by the bed, feeling helpless. The woman stirred. Still alive.

I thought about all the women like her, suffering in obscurity, unable to access life-saving care that I had always considered routine. I vowed to change this.

I described the desperate hospital conditions in an email to my husband, Hal Aronson, who had taught solar energy technology in

California for more than ten years. Hal immediately focused on solar power as a way to provide electricity to the hospital.

When I returned home to Berkeley, Hal sketched a design for a solar electric system to help the Nigerian hospital. He recommended installing stand-alone solar electric systems targeting four parts of the hospital important to maternal survival: the maternity ward, the labour room, the operating room, and the laboratory, where we would install a solar blood bank refrigerator. In each system, solar panels would generate electricity that would be stored in a sealed lead-acid battery for night time use. The system had a charge controller to regulate electricity going into and out of the battery, as well as a load centre to power appliances. Included were 12V DC lights, a charging station for walkie-talkies, and power for other devices, such as surgical suction in the operating room and a blood bank refrigerator in the laboratory. With these systems, labouring women – and their care providers – would no longer have to be in darkness.

The project was compelling, but we needed funds. A campus-wide competition at UC Berkeley advertised a $12,500 grand prize for a technology offering a social good. The deadline for a proposal was eleven days after my return from Nigeria, and provided great incentive to draft a paper and engage the talents of two other Berkeley graduate students: Melissa Ho, from the IT department, and Christian Casillas, from Energy Resources Group. I submitted a 'white paper' on our project and crossed my fingers. A few weeks later, we learned that our project was one of twelve finalists. All of us joined forces to prepare a poster for the competition finals. Melissa and I, along with my seven-year-old daughter, Rachel, dressed in African fashion at the event as we displayed a solar panel, two-way radios, and photos of scenes I had observed at the Nigerian hospital. Our efforts yielded an honourable mention, which carried a $1,000 award, but it wasn't enough to fund my dream.

I came home from the competition, dejected, and called Nigeria to speak to Dr Muazu, the head of Kofan Gayan Hospital. 'We didn't win enough money to do the project,' I apologised. Dr Muazu was unfazed. 'Don't worry, Laura,' he assured me. 'You planted a seed, and from this a great tree will grow.'

A few hours later, I received a call from Thomas Kalil, a campus official who had been at the competition. 'You should have won,' he told me. 'How much do you need for your project?' I knew that our true budget exceeded the competition prize, and hastily doubled the amount originally offered as the grand prize. Within three weeks, Kalil had found us funding through two campus organisations – The Blum Center for Developing Economies and Berkeley Big Ideas.

We could start. The project that would later become We Care Solar had begun.

We set to work mapping out the details of our installation. Our plan was to hire a Nigerian solar company to install solar equipment using Hal's design. We conducted research over the Internet, contacted seven companies, interviewed key representatives by phone, and arranged to meet with one promising solar installer in Nigeria.

I wanted to include my Nigerian hospital colleagues in our planning. Would they like to use walkie-talkies for mobile communication to reduce delays in assembling a surgical team? Would the LED lights we found be bright enough for surgery? Would doctors and nurses find our headlamps (powered with rechargeable batteries) acceptable for clinical care? Their responses would guide our design.

As I planned a return trip to Nigeria I wanted something tangible to show my colleagues – something compact enough to fit in my suitcase. I didn't want the hassle (or potential danger) of explaining our project to customs officials at Abuja airport. I needed this to be discreet.

Hal's solution was a demonstration solar kit to bring on my next journey. He packed my suitcase with compact solar panels, a solar electric control board, a sealed battery, high-efficiency LED lights, headlamps and walkie-talkies. And he invited me to take a workshop on solar energy that he was teaching to educators.

When I returned to Nigeria, I unpacked the case in front of the surgical staff and hospital administrator. I attached the wires and plugged in the battery as Hal had taught me. A doctor flipped the switch and the lights turned on, bringing wide smiles to the hospital staff. The light was indeed bright enough for an operating room. The rechargeable walkie-talkies meant that a surgical team could be assembled in minutes instead of hours, avoiding lengthy searches for doctors and surgical technicians on the hospital grounds. The headlamps with rechargeable batteries were immediately put to use.

*Unpacking the first Solar Suitcase in a Nigerian*
*hospital. Photo courtesy of We Care Solar.*

I met with the Nigerian solar installer whom Hal and I had interviewed by phone, and together we surveyed the hospital, measuring the power requirements for various medical devices. Dr Muazu approved of our plans for a larger installation in six months. But one operating room technician, Aminu Abdullahi, had another idea.

'You must leave your suitcase here,' he insisted. 'This will help us save lives now.' Aminu convinced me that he would care for Hal's equipment in my absence. Indeed, Aminu took charge of the solar devices, dutifully setting the solar panel outside each morning, taking it in at night, and using the system to keep batteries charged for headlamps and two-way radios. The first We Care Solar Suitcase had found a home.

Six months later, I returned to conduct the larger hospital installation, including procurement of a blood bank refrigerator for the laboratory. The hospital was immediately transformed. Midwives could perform obstetric procedures throughout the night, surgical teams were assembled in minutes rather than hours, Caesarean sections were conducted regardless of time of day, and patients were no longer turned away for lack of power. We celebrated the solar installation with a community event, including a ribbon-cutting ceremony from the Kaduna State Minister of Health. Though the hospital staff was clearly pleased with their facility upgrade, staff at one nearby medical clinic felt left out.

'We conduct deliveries in the dark as well,' the clinic manager lamented. 'Why are you only helping the hospital?'

I was initially a bit defensive, explaining that we only had funds for the hospital. However, it soon occurred to me that the suitcase-size system Hal had made for the hospital demonstration could be transplanted to the clinic. We brought the cobbled-together system to the clinic, much to the delight of midwives who no longer needed to rely on candles and kerosene at night.

*Bringing an early Solar Suitcase prototype to a Nigerian clinic. Photo courtesy of We Care Solar.*

I continued to conduct research at Kofan Gayan hospital, returning every few months to observe care. It wasn't long before additional local clinics asked for the 'solar doctor' and the suitcase that would light up maternity care. Hal was glad to accommodate these requests, and started assembling small solar kits for each clinic. On each trip to Nigeria, I would include a Solar Suitcase or two in my luggage.

Word continued to spread, and I was invited to talk about our experience at several US conferences. At one of these meetings, New York Times writer Nicholas Kristof gave a stirring keynote address. After his talk, I told him how his own articles had inspired our work in Africa. The next day, Kristof wrote about our mission in his online blog, and requests for We Care Solar Suitcases arrived from around the world. The need for reliable electricity for maternal health care extended far beyond Nigeria.

Each time I returned to Nigeria I visited the clinics using our solar equipment, making note of any failures as well as the successes. Incorporating feedback from our field installations, the design of our Solar Suitcases became increasingly refined. The suitcase components became more rugged and easier to use. Bare wires needing screwdrivers for installation were replaced with plug-and-play connectors. Safety fuses were replaced with breaker switches. Our simple wooden board was swapped for a plastic panel. And seeing how dirty our equipment became after months of use prompted us to enclose our components in a plastic protective case.

Hal enlisted local volunteers to help with assembly in our backyard. Soon, our Solar Suitcases were travelling to midwives in Burma, clinics in Tibet, and doctors in Tanzania. Solar Suitcases would reach their destination by volunteer couriers who would arrive at our home for training, and then personally transport a Solar Suitcase to a remote clinic or hospital.

When the devastating Haiti earthquake struck in 2010, we had no choice but to get Solar Suitcases into the field as quickly as possible. Medical relief groups made numerous requests for our portable solar power stations, and many small donations poured in as well. In four days, Hal had assembled a team of volunteers to assemble the Solar Suitcases, which we promptly dispatched to several medical groups.

As the Solar Suitcase was introduced to new countries, we worked to adapt the suitcase configuration to meet local requirements.

*Hal Aronson leading the backyard assembly of*
*Solar Suitcases for Haiti. Photo by author.*

Sometimes we learned the hard way. We discovered, for example, that an initial design short-cut – using an American AC-style outlet for our DC lights in Nigeria – was confusing in Haiti, where AC wall outlets accepted (and overpowered) our 12V DC lamps. We redesigned the outlets, and I flew to Haiti with a volunteer engineer, Brent Moellenberg, to retrofit our Solar Suitcases with the new design.

After our experience in Haiti, it became clear to us that our programme was gaining traction. Hal and I dived into the project, converting our home into a Solar Suitcase assembly line. Equipment was strewn all over the house and the living room became our shipping and packing line. We juggled a steady stream of part-time volunteers, including many who were quite talented, but none who could sustain a hefty long-term commitment without remuneration.

Eager to gain increased exposure and support, we entered several competitions, enlisting the support of a talented UC Berkeley MBA student, Abhay Nihalani, and a recent MBA graduate from Duke, Michael MacHarg. In 2010 we applied for (and won) ten competitions and fellowships, including the Global Social Benefit Competition at UC Berkeley, the Ashoka Changemakers Healthy Mothers, Strong World Award, the Global Social Benefit Incubator at Santa Clara University, and a PopTech Fellowship.

This whirlwind year brought me into contact with other social entrepreneurs and mentors, and helped me gain perspective about ways to extend our reach. As I shared our limited experience in Nigeria and Haiti with social entrepreneur groups, we were asked to scale up our operations.

Hal and I had no experience in this realm. Hal had been a solar educator for years, initially creating hands-on solar electricity projects for students, and later, developing a curriculum for educators. My career in medicine demanded clinical and surgical acumen, not project management skills. We needed a thoughtful approach to scale up.

Some advisers suggested the best approach would be mass production of a simplified prototype. They encouraged us to immediately strip down some of the more costly features of our early design, and to manufacture a cheaper, less ambitious version of our product. 'Fewer bells and whistles', we were told.

We were worried about this approach. We had used an iterative approach, evolving the design of the Solar Suitcase to meet the needs of health workers working in unfathomable conditions. We didn't want to downgrade the functionality of our product, and we weren't ready to commit to one particular design without more field research.

Our dream was to create an optimised version of the suitcase incorporating existing feedback from our field installations, and to conduct further research on this model in a limited number of health facilities. Since our formative experience began in northern Nigeria, we thought this would be a good testing site. But we knew this would require staff, time and money.

We applied for independent non-profit status. The recognition we received through awards and fellowships helped us with donations. We got our biggest boost when The MacArthur Foundation funded us specifically to bring our innovation to scale. In awarding us a coveted grant, the foundation recognised the potential for our Solar Suitcases to 'bring light' to an area of maternal health care that had previously been largely ignored. Our grant targeted four areas – technology design, educational programming, field research, and scale-up of operations. With this funding, and additional research support from the Blum Center for Developing Economies, we could hire key personnel, and we were on our way.

Our learning curve was steep. We had never run a non-profit organisation, managed international programmes, or interacted with contract manufacturers and government officials. We asked for help wherever we could find it, thankful to receive mentorship from business consultants, lawyers, industrial engineers, designers, social entrepreneurs and academics. We are fortunate to be based in the San Francisco Bay Area, which enabled us to collaborate with a diverse talent pool: students and professors from UC Berkeley and Stanford, scientists from Lawrence Berkeley National Laboratory, other technology-oriented non-profits, and advisers from Silicon Valley.

Hal and I devoted ourselves full time to We Care Solar. We hired consultants to help lead operations and provide financial oversight.

*Brent Moellenberg, Hal Aronson and Christian Casillas preparing version 2.0 of the Solar Suitcase. Photo by author.*

109

Brent Moellenberg, the engineer who had led our technical activities in Haiti, was brought on board full time. As our organisational capacity expanded, we developed systems for accounting, data management and inventory. Hal and Brent met with lighting designers, solar manufacturers and contract manufacturers. Our aim was to 'design for manufacturability,' which meant making user-friendly, rugged Solar Suitcases in a factory rather than our house! We found that our mission – to use solar light and power to improve maternal health – attracted generous in-kind support. So we were able to accomplish a great deal with a limited budget.

We realised that the technology alone was not sustainable without proper usage and long-term maintenance. In addition to developing photo-rich user manuals, we printed bright laminated posters, recognising from our site visits that in rural clinics, posters were the most common form of written information. We created educational programmes for health workers, and a basic curriculum on solar energy and optimal use of the Solar Suitcase. We prepared more advanced materials on installation and maintenance for technicians. And we piloted this programme in Liberia with sixty health providers, before

*Training Nigerian health workers to use the Solar Suitcase. Photo courtesy of We Care Solar.*

extending the programme to Nigeria, Sierra Leone, Uganda and Malawi.

As we travelled from country to country, we conducted facility assessments at diverse health centres, which exposed us to variations of health facility layout, construction materials and energy needs. As a result of our research, we expanded the capacity of the Solar Suitcase, and included hardware and tools to facilitate installation. Our newer version accommodated larger panels and batteries, included a foetal heart rate monitor, and had the option for additional lights that could be plugged into a 'satellite' receptacle.

We interviewed health workers before and after they used the Solar Suitcases, and monitored system performance with electronic data loggers.

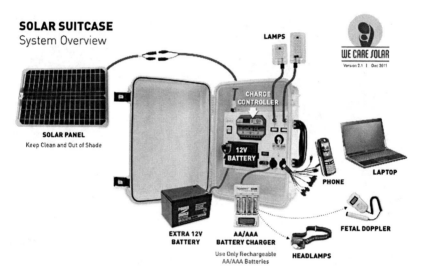

*Poster of the Solar Suitcase; this is used in the training curriculum. Photo courtesy of We Care Solar.*

Midwives told us of how they previously struggled to provide care at night by using candles, kerosene lanterns, or cellphone lights. At times, they were forced to hold their only light source in their mouths to keep both hands free for medical care. Perhaps the most striking example came from a Nigerian midwife who was unable to finish a delivery in the dark. There was no kerosene, no candle, nothing to provide light in her clinic. In desperation, she asked her assistant to set a match to the calendar on the wall, and she finished the delivery by the glow of the burning paper.

We learned that Solar Suitcases enabled health workers to perform procedures throughout the night. Specifically, midwives explained that it was easier to conduct routine and complicated deliveries, treat bleeding mothers, administer medication at night, keep phones charged for emergency referrals, and resuscitate newborn babies. Many clinics stayed open longer hours, and patients were more likely to seek skilled care in a facility that they knew had light. We heard again and again that reliable lighting and phone charging improved health worker morale and reduced the fear that used to go hand-in-hand with working in a darkened health centre.

*Liberian health workers receiving a Solar
Suitcase at night. Photo by author.*

We have been surprised to receive requests for Solar Suitcases from large maternity wards and hospital operating theatres in need of reliable power. Even though we explain that our Solar Suitcases have a limited light supply not intended for larger rooms, hospital administrators insist that our Solar Suitcase lighting is vastly superior to the candles and kerosene lanterns that are the only source of lighting when the power grid is down. The Solar Suitcase is seen as an essential back-up source of power to the utility grid.

Indeed, when we visited eastern Uganda in the summer of 2012 to assess the impact of the Solar Suitcase, I was privy to a night-time Caesarean section during which the main power stopped functioning. With a Solar Suitcase light above the operating table, the surgery continued without interruption. The doctors told us the Solar Suitcase lights were better for surgery than their usual lights, and there was no longer the need to send patients to distant hospitals when night falls.

We now have more than 400 suitcases in over twenty-five countries, helping tens of thousands of women give birth more safely every year. Each small success has been celebrated, but is often supplanted by an array of new tasks and responsibilities of larger magnitude. The biggest challenge has been in designing programmes to scale up distribution and maintenance in countries with poor physical and political infrastructure. We are now partnering with NGOs and UN agencies such as the World Health Organisation (WHO), the United Nations Population Fund (UNFPA) and UNICEF to implement our programmes.

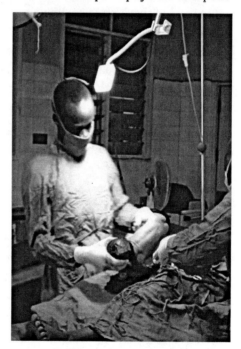

Sometimes the pressure feels overwhelming – we have a limited staff and we are tackling an enormous problem. It would be so much easier to ignore the problem of energy poverty in health care. As we approach our breaking point, we often receive an inspiring story of how the Solar Suitcase is helping a health provider, or a clinic, or saving a life.

*A Ugandan surgeon uses a Solar Suitcase light to conduct an emergency C-section. Photo courtesy of Jacqueline Cutts.*

One such story came from Dr Jacques Sebisaho, a New York-trained doctor who operates a clinic on the island of Idjwi in the Democratic Republic of the Congo. The village has no power and, when night falls, it is impossible to provide adequate medical care. On this trip, the doctor had a Solar Suitcase, which was quickly put to use to illuminate a twin delivery.

More alarming, his arrival coincided with the onset of a cholera epidemic. The clinic was flooded with patients needing intravenous fluids, antibiotics and constant monitoring. The clinic could not house all the patients in need of care, and mats were placed outside on the ground, creating a makeshift outdoor infirmary. The Solar Suitcase lighting was brought from patient to patient, and enabled the team to provide constant monitoring.

Although Dr Sebisaho feared many lives could be lost, he and his team achieved something they considered a near-miracle. All 122 patients treated that month survived – not a single man, woman or child was lost despite the severity of many of the cases. He had expected 50% of the patients to die, and said that 80% of deaths occur at night.

In the case of Dr Sebisaho, the Solar Suitcase was a lifesaver, boosting the morale of health workers and inspiring the entire community.

> *I believe the light was the force behind everything. I have no words to describe how confident we all were, knowing we could do anything anytime (day or night). This sounds obvious to a person here [in the USA], but the light meant the world there.*
>
> *We are witnessing what light can do in a community and how it can save lives in regions where night means death if [you are] sick or in need of emergency care after the sun goes down!*

The stories of Dr Sebisaho, and hundreds of midwives, nurses and doctors who are grateful for the light they need to do their work, infuse us with the energy we need to continue our journey. So despite the sacrifices, the endless challenges, the constant stream of work ahead, we continue to move forward.

Just as I could not have predicted how my life would unfold at seventeen when I was a dancer and pianist, nor at forty when I could no longer continue my beloved medical practice, so too I cannot predict the journey that lies ahead for We Care Solar. What I do know is that every day women and their infants are struggling in childbirth in the dark, in remote (and not so remote) corners of the world. And beyond the health clinics there are orphanages, schools, refugee camps and other institutions where human needs are compromised because of a lack of reliable electricity.

*Dr Jacques Sebisaho (just right of centre) on Idjwi Island introducing the Solar Suitcase. Photo courtesy of Jacques Sebisaho.*

With the Solar Suitcase, I know that we have the power to change that. And as long as We Care Solar and Hal and I are here, we will continue our efforts to harness the power of the sun to improve people's lives.

## ACKNOWLEDGEMENTS

My life partner, Hal Aronson, was the driving force behind the Solar Suitcase. From the moment I shared my observations of the effects of energy poverty in a Nigerian hospital, Hal dedicated himself to developing a solution for this problem. In addition to being the true innovator

# 6

## THE POWER OF TOUCH

### Louisa Silva

*Observing how well the autistic son of a close friend
responds to the therapeutic effects of a Chinese massage
technique that she has advocated using, Louisa Silva
is convinced that the treatment has the potential to
benefit thousands of others, but she needs to prove it.*

Sometimes, it is only when a condition starts to get better that you understand what was wrong in the first place. Such has been my experience with autism. As I came to find out, the solution was in the problem.

I am a doctor of Western and Chinese medicines, with a further specialty in public health. Throughout my appointment at Western Oregon University's Teaching Research Institute I have researched a massage treatment for young children with autism that is based on principles of Chinese medicine.

I didn't start my medical career with a desire to do university-based research. In fact, I came to it later in life, after I turned fifty. My first passion was public health. The mission to help people stay healthy – and when they are ill, to give them safe, affordable treatment – is the one that drew me to medicine, and one I really believe in to this day.

I've worked internationally in Central America and India, as well as in the United States, and over the years as I reached the limits of what Western medicine could do for my patients, I added osteopathic medicine, homeopathic medicine and herbal medicine to my repertoire. It wasn't until I studied Chinese medicine, however, that I hit the proverbial jackpot for safe and effective treatments. I had already integrated the principles of Chinese medicine into my family medical practice in Salem, Oregon and was contentedly practising my particular blend of Chinese medicine, public health and Western medicine, when in 2000 something happened that took my life in a totally unexpected direction.

## THE CALL FOR HELP

The son of a dear friend wasn't developing normally. He was four and he hadn't started talking. He wasn't sleeping (and so his parents weren't sleeping either). He was hyperactive, constantly running around – and running off. He was easily overstimulated to the point of meltdown. Even ordinary family events like meals, gatherings, or outings were major struggles. Despite the fact that both parents were educators and skilled communicators, they couldn't communicate with him, teach him, or even reach him most of the time. It was difficult for them to moderate his energy or regulate his behaviour. He could not be soothed or redirected. Simply keeping him from being a danger to himself was an exhausting, all-consuming task.

I had been aware of the difficulties my friends had endured – how many months they'd spent visiting specialists to find out what was wrong, how hard it was for them to get through each day. But when the diagnosis of autism finally came, what caught me square between the eyes was how little relief this 'answer' brought them. Instead, the information sent my friends into a tailspin of despair that dragged the whole family down.

Up to this point it had taken all of my friends' energy to keep their son contained and safe. Neither they nor the boy's sister were having their needs met. My friends had been running on fumes, waiting for the diagnosis and treatment that could finally help them. But when the doctors gave them that diagnosis, their hope evaporated. Autism is a lifelong disability. There is no known cause. There is no known cure. In short, they were told that there was nothing they could do. The only treatment was the early intervention services he was already receiving.

I couldn't just stand by and watch my friends suffer through an unbearable situation. I remembered watching my Chinese medicine professor, Dr Anita Cignolini, give a massage to a four-year-old autistic boy. Within a few days worth of massages he had begun to make eye contact with her and could roll a ball back and forth to her. I thought that this massage technique might help my friends' son.

Dr Cignolini's treatment incorporated qigong massage, which works on restoring the flow of qi (vital energy) through the major energy channels in the body. The idea that we can restore health and improve circulation by working with these energy channels has been the basis of Chinese medicine for 3,000 years. Dr Cignolini designed her autism massage treatment based on her own experiences and her studies with a qigong master from China.

I flew to California and typed while she dictated the protocol. The massage is a series of eleven movements administered by a doctor trained in both Western and Chinese medicines. It takes about 15 minutes to massage the child down the energy channels of the body from head to toe. The doctor advances the cause by giving the expert version of the massage ten times over five weeks, while the parents, who learn the treatment from the doctor, maintain the gains by giving the massage at home daily.

When I returned home I taught the treatment to my friends. We tried it on their son and it worked. He calmed down, his behaviour became more manageable, and in turn my friends calmed down and were able to pull out of their emotional tailspin. And then it came to me – there were thousands of children and parents whom this massage could help, but no one would ever believe me if I went around saying that you could treat a neurological disorder like autism with massage, albeit a very specialised massage. I was going to have to prove this scientifically.

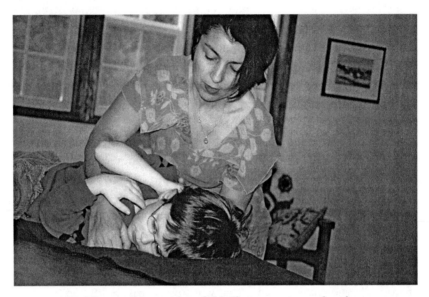

*Dr Silva working with a child. Photo courtesy of author.*

At the time I was completing a Masters in Public Health and Preventive Medicine at Western Oregon University. A few years previously I had started another clinic to serve the local immigrant population. We were integrating Western and Chinese medicine approaches to find affordable, effective means of treating complicated chronic illnesses. The timing was perfect. I needed a research project for my degree, and no research had been done on qigong massage for autism. Here was my thesis project literally in my hands.

## EARLY RESEARCH

I contacted the local intervention services for the autism programme, and without endorsing the project they helped me locate eight subjects. An occupational therapist and a speech therapist volunteered their services to do the pre- and post-treatment testing for autism, behaviour and development. I taught the parents of the test subjects and met them weekly to support the home massage component of the programme.

At the end of ten weeks the children were more social, made more eye contact, and were eating and sleeping better, and the parents were less stressed. All of the developmental measures had improved. The occupational therapist reported that the children were easier to touch, which would later prove to be a vital clue towards unravelling the puzzle of autism. The confusion between touch and pain, the way the senses didn't seem to work together, the lack of eye contact, and the reasons why the normal methods that parents employ to calm young children using touch didn't work in autism would start to make sense.

I finished my Masters programme and submitted the pilot study for publication in a British autism journal. The reviewers turned it down – somewhat snidely, I thought – questioning my background and telling me the article wasn't up to their standards. I resubmitted the manuscript to an alternative journal, the *American Journal of Chinese Medicine*, and this time it was accepted. It was my first lesson in the difficulty of publishing alternative research in mainstream journals.

The experience didn't temper my desire to get the word out, though. I didn't want to be sidelined as 'alternative'. The massage treatment needed to be in mainstream early intervention programmes. I realised that I was going to have to do more than a case series. I needed to raise the bar and do a controlled study.

Children with autism share certain characteristics, including unusual sensory responses. Their sense of touch is distorted and they feel pain differently than normal children. A child with autism can be oversensitive to touch on one part of the body, not register pain on another, and respond normally to touch on a third area. Their ears aren't tuned to pick up the human voice, and they might pay lots of attention to a distant mechanical noise and none to the voices of their siblings. The senses of taste and smell are affected, and children with autism may only eat a very small variety of foods. Their eyes don't seek the human face, and they don't make eye contact. With the next study, I wanted to investigate more thoroughly how these symptoms changed in response to the massage.

I learned to write grant proposals. Eight applications and seven rejections later, I was awarded a small grant. None of the autism groups had been interested in my case series – it was a local Native American casino, Spirit Mountain Community Fund, which offered funding. This seemed fitting to me, as Native American culture emphasises energy and spirit. The scientific groups funding autism research were only interested in genetic research and technical solutions at that time, and qigong massage simply didn't fit the profile.

I recruited fifteen children, randomised them into two groups, and carried out a small controlled study, this time for twice as long. Parents gave the massage daily for five months, and I provided support and massage weekly. I gave 300 massages throughout the course of the study. We did pre- and post-treatment testing for sensory problems, autism severity and developmental measures. As before, we saw behaviour and language improvement, and very clearly improved sensory responses. All the senses started responding more normally, but the changes in touch were the most dramatic. The skin is the largest sensory organ: touch is the mother of all senses.

It was fascinating to see what happened with the children's hands. We experience so much of the world through our hands. We identify objects with our hands, we shake hands to greet, we hold hands with those we love. As Chinese medicine texts say, our hands are connected to our hearts. It was very difficult to touch the children's fingers at first. They would pull their hands away as if they were in pain. But within a few weeks of starting the massage, I could see their fingers relax, and they would begin to use their index fingers to point. They would look at their hands being massaged and then look at me. What was it about hands?

Autistic children aren't social, and I delved into this fact for clues about why the massage was working. I started reading about shared traits between mammals, social creatures that require the presence of other social creatures in order to survive a long, dependent growing-up period. We nurse, we bond, we have a four-chambered heart and twelve cranial nerves. There is a brilliant new theory of the mammal social brain that you won't find in the textbooks, but you will find in thousands of research papers. It explains that deep in our brainstem we have an ancient reptilian brain that switches into fight-or-flight mode whenever survival is threatened. But our survival also depends on being social. And we have a newer mammalian social brainstem that helps us learn to be social that is switched on by touch. Every time we are held, nursed, and cared for by our parents, this brainstem is activated and exercised. Without touch, it remains out of commission, but with touch, it sends messages in three directions simultaneously: to our heart to calm down, to our head, eyes and ears, to face, look at and listen to one another, and to the social engagement part of our brain, to be receptive to communication. This is the nuts and bolts of how touch helps us learn to be social, and this is what wasn't working in autism. I knew this theory could explain autism and the success of the massage treatment, but it wasn't an accepted theory of autism.

Now I was really in trouble. I knew there were millions of children with autism worldwide, and I had proof that the massage worked, but apart from Dr Cignolini, who was by now retired in Sicily, and myself in Oregon, there were no other practitioners anywhere else in the world. How were we going to provide the treatment to the people who needed it?

In Dr Cignolini's view, the massage had to be administered by a Western physician who was also trained in Chinese medicine. In the USA there are only a handful of such doctors in each State. Given that they already had busy practices, who was to say that I could recruit them to learn how to treat autistic children? Working with these children can be chaotic, physical, emotionally draining and just plain hard at first. Imagine trying to massage a kicking, screaming, four-year-old who does not want you to touch even the top of his head. I knew I wouldn't be able to persuade this group to change their practices to focus on just one population. Besides, even if they all jumped on board, there still wouldn't be enough of them to meet the need.

I had to find a group of trainees who had enough experience with autism to be able to get their hands on the children and work with them, and who understood the emotional territory of autism well enough to make good connections with the parents and support them. The early intervention people fitted the description. They were already working with children and supporting parents, and they were desperate for tools.

This might sound like a great solution, but it created all sorts of conflicts for me personally. Was I really going to train early intervention therapists in Chinese medicine? In China, qigong massage is considered medical therapy to be given by doctors trained in Chinese medicine. Was it time to step off the beaten path and try something new? I decided to develop an Applied Chinese Medicine curriculum to teach the autism treatment to Western early intervention therapists. It was a very creative project and I had a lot of fun bringing the ancient concepts of Chinese medicine to life for non-practitioners. I was sharing the wealth, and it was wonderful to put healing tools in their hands.

I pulled together a group of therapists, trained them, tested their results against my own, and determined that the curriculum approach did work. Western early intervention therapists could achieve the same good results with children as a trained Chinese medicine doctor. We were all set. We had identified the group of people we could train to disseminate the massage to the parents. Additionally, the study was accepted for publication in a mainstream journal, the *American Journal of Occupational Therapy*. We could start to roll the research out to the mainstream early intervention professionals we wanted to reach.

In the meantime, the parents and professionals who participated in the research studies helped me understand something key. While the research played an important role in encouraging the parents to start the massage treatment – they needed some sort of proof that it worked for autism – motivating the parents to carry out the programme every day required much more. It required 'seeing is believing'. After all, here was a therapy that was only successful if parents played their part. Without daily massage, the children didn't get better. With daily massage, they got better, and better, and better. We started with five months of daily massage in our studies, but what we soon realised is that parents actually needed to continue the treatment for a year for it to be fully successful. And no parent is going to massage her child every day for a year unless she sees her kid getting better. It didn't matter whether parents were complete sceptics or true believers; it only mattered that they saw steady (if gradual) improvement at the start. Once families saw the treatment work, they believed in it. And once they believed they had the power to help their child, they would do anything to help.

# A Theory for Autism

Every research study seemed to lead to a new one, and I kept refining the massage itself. There were now twelve movements in the sequence, each one could be done in several ways, and there were back-up techniques in case the child refused or avoided touch to specific areas. Five years into this, projects were multiplying like rabbits. I had started out doing one research study at a time, and now I had several going simultaneously. During the first three studies I had observed a lot of kids very closely under my own hands and captured hundreds of treatment sessions for video analysis. Because I was looking at the children through the lens of Chinese medicine, I was noticing predictable symptoms that were not part of the standard definition of autism.

Let's take a moment to review the standard definition of autism. It is based on the appearance of these things by the age of three – the absence (or delayed development) of social skills, the absence (or delayed development) of language, and the presence of odd, repetitive behaviours. Nobody really knew the reason for these traits. Why didn't social and language skills develop normally? Why was behaviour so odd and repetitive?

The predictable symptoms I was tracking were those present most of the time, in most of the kids – tantrums and meltdowns, sleep problems, appetite and digestion problems, problems with eye contact, and most strikingly, problems with touch. It seemed that these symptoms might be able to explain why social skills didn't develop normally, and why the children's behaviour was so disconnected from what was happening around them. These problems aren't unique to autism – they occur in other children, too – but they are extremely common in children with autism and seem to be much more severe. (In addition, these symptoms are extremely disturbing to parents, which make them very important in the treatment picture.) The autism research literature calls them co-morbid symptoms, and writes them off – unknown cause, unknown significance.

The massage was improving these other symptoms and, as they improved, the standard autism symptoms improved. We had the massage refined to the point where we knew which massage movement could ameliorate which symptom. After looking at more than a thousand hours of video, I was convinced that there was meaning and significance to the way children reacted to touch on different parts of the body. For example, problems with touch on the ears translated to difficulty listening and delayed language. Problems with touch on the chest meant an inability to self-soothe and a greater disposition towards tantrums and meltdowns. Problems with touch on the belly signified diarrhoea or constipation. There was a geography of meaning on the skin.

Once we figured out how to adapt the massage to make the child's responses on the different areas comfortable and normal, the symptoms would get better. If we didn't avoid the ears, and instead stayed on them and worked through the difficulty, the child would start to use his ears to listen, and language would follow. If we massaged the chest for several minutes until the child started to rub his eyes and yawn, he would start to self-soothe, and tantrums and meltdowns would disappear. We could change the direction of massage on the belly so that we could help alleviate either constipation or diarrhoea. This was wonderful and powerful stuff. Parents were amazed at what they could do, but at the same time they were saying 'It feels so natural'. And it was. Touch is natural. Chinese medicine is natural medicine.

By 2007 I had a theory for autism that I needed to test. And then to satisfy the mainstream scientific community, I needed to do a still-larger controlled study. But first, I had to create tools to measure the co-morbid symptoms and their improvements. Although there were many of these symptoms, and each child started out with different combinations of them, I had seen that over the course of five months they had all improved in predictable ways. This information needed to be disseminated to other professionals working with children with autism, which meant more studies.

The skin became an important part of my theory. Each child had a different and strange combination of under-sensitive, over-sensitive and normal skin. The same child who might pull away at the touch of a parent's hand might not even notice a bleeding gash on their leg. Instead of having a clear, clean boundary telling them where they end, and where the rest of the world begins, autistic children receive a confused mixture of disorganised sensations from their skin. No wonder they are on edge!

With the massage there was a predictable progression from numbness to hypersensitivity to normal sensation and then the skin started working as a cohesive sensory organ rather than a collection of scattered parts. Suddenly it made sense to me that the children didn't use the word 'I' – there wasn't a clear sense of self. Once the massage started, however, their skin would normalise, and parents would report that children were starting to use 'I'. With a sense of self came self-expression. And then the real child, who was inside all the time, could come out.

It was always a milestone when the children felt pain from a real injury for the first time. It seemed to trigger something deeper. Once they could feel pain, they could shed tears that conveyed their own emotions, and then they could feel empathy for someone else's pain. If one of their siblings fell down and cried, they would be concerned about whether or not she was okay. Before, when they didn't notice their own pain, they didn't notice anyone else's either.

Even time was coded into the skin, namely onto the back. The past is behind us. So is our back. We noticed that children who were numb on their backs didn't use them – they couldn't turn onto their backs when asked, and didn't respond to being tapped on the back. These same children had no idea what had happened earlier that day. Once the massage restored normal sensation to the back, the children could turn over when asked, and lo and behold, they could describe what had happened in school that day, and what they had eaten for lunch. They acquired a past. And once they acquired a past, they could have a future, and could participate in and understand planning conversations, such as which day they had swimming lessons, or when the family was going to Grandma's. It was fascinating.

With the recovery of a whole skin and the emergence of a time and place for self, came self-regulation. It is a fact that human development rests solidly on the development of early self-regulatory abilities. I found a paper describing the four self-regulation milestones in the first year of life. Similar to the motor milestones of sitting up, standing and walking, there are definite self-regulation milestones that lay the foundation for later development, namely:

- The ability to have regular sleep.
- The ability to have a regular appetite and digestion.
- The ability to self-soothe.
- The ability to orient and pay attention.

As I had noted, the children with whom we were working were delayed in all of these areas. It now made sense that the social milestones normally in place by age three did not develop. How could a child learn social skills without being able to calm down, make eye contact and pay attention to the people around them? It was time to design and validate a research measure or two to capture this.

It turns out that there is a touch barrier in autism. My studies showed that children with autism are different than other children by virtue of an abnormal, patchy sense of touch on their skin. This was behind the difficulties in self-regulating and the social delay. The difficult behaviours were the result of confusing and conflicting information about the world outside their skin, and the body in which they lived. Without clear information to give them a sense of who and where they were, how could they regulate themselves? And when their nervous system triggered fight-or-flight responses at inappropriate times, how could they calm down if the very thing that was supposed to calm them down – touch – triggered fight-or-flight? And, without touch – that is to say, without a properly functioning skin – they were not going to learn to self-soothe and enjoy being social. It became obvious why the massage worked. It broke the touch barrier.

## A SECOND WIND

Over the next five years I embarked on more controlled studies and continued to train therapists and refine the training materials. We treated hundreds of children all over Oregon, and published the results in mainstream journals. (I will always thank the *American Journal of Occupational Therapy* for seeing the value of this work early on, and for being willing to disseminate it to occupational therapists.) I started a non-profit, the Qigong Sensory Training Institute. A friend put together a website for parents and professionals (qsti.org) and we started presenting the research at national and international conferences. The project now took up every available minute I had apart from working at my clinic and raising my daughter. Emotionally, I found it extraordinarily satisfying – it was a deep honour to be involved in this work. Physically, I found it exhausting. I knew how I got into this work, but how was I ever going to get out?

I needed an exit plan, but there were still so many children who needed help. I couldn't run out of gas now. I had to have something irrefutable and portable to give to these families and practitioners before I could go my own way. My sister, who is a tech-wizard, reorganised the website, and all of a sudden we were showing up on the first page of Google searches on autism treatment for children. Emails started coming in from all over the world from parents who wanted instructions on how to do the massage. People were asking for a book and a DVD. I had only one option – I had to redouble my efforts! With the editing support of my neighbour and dear friend, Kristi Negri, I wrote a book, *Qigong Massage for Your Child with Autism: A Home Program from Chinese Medicine*. Another dear friend, Donna Read, created a training DVD to go with the book, and made a short documentary film about a group of families in rural Oregon who were implementing the massage at home. So, we had done it – we had created training materials for parents who wanted them. But what kind of results could parents achieve on their own?

By 2012 we had published ten studies on treating children under the age of six. The results were consistent in all of the studies. After five months of daily parent massage and twenty therapist massages – averaging one a week – children were about 30% improved. The severely autistic children moved into the moderate range, the moderate children moved into the mild range, and some of the mildly affected children moved off the autism spectrum altogether. As the skin became normal, the child could calm down and pay attention, the social parts of the brain began to learn better and the autism became less severe. It wasn't a cure, but it definitely helped.

We had done two studies in which only the parents implemented the massage, not the therapists, and it was clear that parents could accomplish a lot if they were given sufficient training and support. With the severely autistic children parents could obtain about half the results that parents and therapists could achieve working together, but the same was true for therapists working without the support of the parents. The full benefits seemed to come when parents and therapists worked together, and five months seemed to be enough time for collaboration. In that time span, the children would settle down, and the parents would become competent at the massage and find the motivation to continue it for as long as the child needed it – usually about a year.

## CALMER WATERS

I've crossed a lot of bridges to get to where I am today. When I started, there was no published scientific literature showing the effectiveness of qigong massage treatment for autism. There was no public awareness of qigong massage. There were no theories for autism that included sensory and self-regulatory problems, and no way to measure whether treatment helped sensory and self-regulatory problems. Apart from myself and Dr Cignolini there were no practitioners of qigong massage for autism, and there were no training programmes for practitioners and parents. All of this has been addressed.

My own belief systems have been challenged. Over the years, I've had to rethink three myths that I had been trained to believe, both professionally and culturally. The first is that you have to be a doctor to practice Chinese medicine and assist healing – the early intervention people are doing a great job with the massage. The second is that parents cannot provide treatment for a neurological handicap – no one else but a parent can give the massage day in and day out for a year. The third is that treatment for a serious neurological condition like autism must surely be complicated and expensive – this treatment is both easy to teach and nearly free to dispense.

## BACK TO TOUCH

Through my work with autistic children, I've come to understand the importance of touch to our development as human beings. As a society we've forgotten how much children need to be touched every day and, sadly, with both parents working children are receiving less touch. We undervalue touch or sexualise it. Our school boards, so concerned with avoiding lawsuits, have gone so far as to forbid teachers to touch children at all. Teachers substitute auditory or visual ways of communication, but auditory and visual stimuli don't calm down the nervous system like touch does. With less touch there is less stimulus to self-regulate, and systems that have been set in place for millennia to assure development are not exercised as they are meant to be. The result is that children are more on edge, and they are literally less comfortable in their own skin. Paediatricians' offices are full of children who are irritable and have prolonged tantrums, who don't sleep or eat well, and whose behaviour is difficult for their parents to manage. These children are not diagnosed with autism – they are diagnosed with self-regulatory difficulties and put on medication. (It is mind-boggling how many elementary school children are on medication for anxiety. I think that daily massage could possibly help them, too.)

For young children with autism, touch is a slippery slope. These children don't respond to normal touch with pleasure and relaxation, and tend to refuse touch. Parents don't know what to do. They feel they are doing something wrong, and touch their children less. Before they know it, they've stopped touching their children altogether and are trying to use words or gestures to communicate and calm – which don't work as well on the body as touch. As they receive less touch, children become more irritable and anxious, and their behaviour deteriorates. The further behind children fall socially, the harder it is for them to learn almost everything they need to grow up to be an independent adult. But re-introducing touch, especially as an early intervention technique, can stop this downward spiral.

I've come to appreciate the relationship between touch and eye contact. Both of them are important to parent–child bonding. Touch is a physical connection that allows us to feel and be felt. It is as necessary to the health of a child as breathing. Eye contact is a mental connection that allows us to see and be seen, know and be known. Chinese medicine describes eye contact as a touching of our minds and our spirits. And touch is the first trigger for eye contact. All the time the baby is held and nursed, as long as his eyes are open, he stares unwaveringly at his mother's face. Although children with autism avoid eye contact, it is one of the first things to come back with the massage. I have seen parents weep with relief as they recount that their child is now looking at them, referencing them, acting like they are connected to them. The parent–child bond is energised by a thousand shared hugs and moments of eye contact. The dad shown in the photo to the left was sad every time he tried to show his love for his son with a hug and was refused, and now that his son asks, he treasures the hugs beyond words.

*Father and son embrace.*
*Photo by author.*

The beauty of Chinese medicine is that it knows how to use touch for healing. There are techniques to open up the circulation to the skin using our hands. There are techniques to use touch to help a child go to sleep, or to trigger self-soothing and stop a tantrum. And these help to open up the senses so they all work together to give the child a steady stream of reliable information about their body and the world around them. It takes training and support for parents to go back to touching areas of their child's body that seem to hurt (painful fingers and toes are very common in autism), and it seems counter-intuitive at first, that massaging these areas of discomfort will heal them. But seeing is believing, and the massage does heal them.

The knowledge of Chinese medicine is available to all of us and is the gift of ancient China to all of humanity. It is knowledge that is very close to the bone, about how we can help ourselves and our children grow and heal. It is as ancient as civilisation.

## Coming Full Circle

After years of rejection and scepticism from large granting agencies, ivory tower universities and elite autism journals, qigong massage for autism is gaining credibility. I eventually had an article published in a premier US autism journal. Genetic research has failed to deliver on its promises to reveal the cause of and the cure for autism, and is no longer monopolising autism funding. In July 2012 the Federal Department of Maternal and Child Health offered my university a large grant to treat 120 children over three years – finally, a chance to do the definitive big study that could elevate qigong massage in status from 'promising autism research' to a treatment that will be disseminated to early intervention agencies nationwide. It's the same grant that we failed to secure in 2011. I'm not sure what happened in one year to make them reconsider us, but I suspect that social media had something to do with it. Our Google rankings have never been higher.

I am now less desperate for an exit strategy. My life has calmed down inexplicably, the really hard work has been done, and I have the support of an extraordinary group of friends, parents and colleagues to help with the work as it comes.

What advice would I give to another person who hears the call? Listen to your heart, and ask yourself whether what you have to offer is important and meaningful to other people. If something is calling you hard, and if you really believe in it, then prove it, and put it out there for everyone to see. Do your homework, and work hard. Take care of your own health, especially when you feel tired and it seems like you will never finish the work. Offer yourself choices. When things became really difficult for me and I wanted to bail, I visualised the end of my life, and asked myself if I would be sorry that I didn't further this work. And when the answer came, I made my choice. I've never regretted it. Follow the passion and the love, and listen for guidance. Definitely don't get attached to knowing how things are going to turn out. Remember what Yoda said: 'Trust the Force'.

# THE RIPPLE EFFECT

## Lynn Price

*Haunted by the memory of being separated from her
older sister during a childhood spent in foster care,
and horrified that other siblings are continuing to
suffer the same fate, Lynn Price resolves to devise
a way to bring such people back together.*

*Brothers and sisters: They fight, argue and tease – and yet they are each
other's best advocates, best friends and enjoy the longest relationships
in life.*

Sitting at a courtyard table on the campus of Child Haven, a children's
shelter in Las Vegas, I followed little Emily's gaze across the grassy
quad to a teenage boy shooting baskets on the court across the way.
'Who is he?' I asked. 'My brother, Jimmy,' she answered shyly. 'He looks
like a great basketball player and great big brother,' I said with a smile.
Emily didn't hesitate for a moment. 'He is very cool and I miss him so

much,' she said tearfully. 'Well, let's get him over here,' I cried, rising from the table. I started to walk towards Jimmy to invite him to join us.

That's when a full time staffer approached me and informed me that Jimmy could not come over. As a weekly volunteer, I was unfamiliar with that policy. While the Department of Children and Family Services investigated whether it was safe for the children to return home to their parents, or organised transition to foster care or relatives, children and youths were temporarily assigned to a specific cottage and area of the campus according to age and gender.

Even though they were brother and sister, Emily and Jimmy had to remain in their respective areas of the campus, except during special events that took place from time to time for all children and youths at the shelter.

The thought struck me like a bolt of lightning. Brothers and sisters are being separated and can't get together when they want? I had a personal flashback to when my sister Andi and I were separated in different foster homes and could only see each other on supervised visits or at special events.

Abandoned by our father, and deprived of our mother, who was institutionalised following a mental breakdown, Andi and I were placed into separate foster homes. I was eight months old and Andi was two-and-a-half at the time. It wasn't until I was eight years old that my foster parents revealed they were not my real parents. Evidently, our mother had made a miracle recovery and wanted to see her children. That's when the parents I always called 'mom and dad' told me that they were my foster parents, that I was a foster child, and that I had a 'real' mother and an older sister.

I was stunned, wanted my mom and dad, not another mother, refused to accept the label of 'foster child' or acknowledge an older sister, and hated playing the foster role during the next few years when we had supervised visits or special events.

Things changed when I was a junior in high school and Andi was a freshman in college. She invited me to spend a weekend with her. Excited to go to the big school, yet scared to share a weekend with a stranger, I arrived at campus only to be met by Andi with open arms and a whisper in my ear: 'Can I introduce you as my little sister?'

Wow, after all the years when I did not even acknowledge her, she wanted to call me her little sister and for all her friends to know about me. I was a celebrity on campus. It was the first time we were together for our own special event, without our different parents or the social workers who stood by on all our visits and events. That was the start of our friendship, and a sisterhood that is so close today.

As I explained to Emily that Jimmy could not come over, I couldn't fathom how this kind of separation could still be happening, and on a campus, no less, where they could even see each other across the way. There had been no policies or procedures in place to enable Andi and me to see each other, except for supervised visits and special events. We didn't have a connection, and only came to know each other later in life, at the end of our journey in foster care. In our early years we missed out on all the typical everyday sibling interactions, just like Emily and Jimmy. We didn't have any quality connection.

A seed was planted. How many siblings were separated and how could I find a way to give brothers and sisters quality connection time for typical everyday events while they were in foster care?

My research revealed that out of 500,000 youths in foster care in the USA, 75% were separated from at least one sibling. No fighting over who sits where in the car, sharing secrets, celebrating birthdays, telling on each other, playing hopscotch, helping each other with homework, even going on family vacations together. Andi and I did not have any of those experiences of unconditional love, important family social interaction and shared family memories.

A few days later I overheard a conversation between the sister of one of my best friends and another girl about a camp she started for underprivileged youths. Aha, I thought, how about a camp for brothers and sisters separated by foster care? They could share typical everyday events together, enjoy quality time for connection, without interruption, and create childhood memories as they journeyed through foster care!

I excitedly asked Andi what she thought about a camp for siblings, just siblings, to provide them with the fun times and memories that we did not have. Her quick response was: 'I've never heard of that, but if you say it is going to happen, it will!'

An innovation that seemed like common sense to me, siblings sharing life, took on a life of its own. My intention was just a camp for a few days, as a one-off.

I was an executive in the telecommunications industry leading new and emerging cable networks and had started my own marketing firm. Certainly I understood 'innovative', so I could start a non-profit for siblings, too. I had the gift of the gab as an inspirational speaker and was penning my first book. I didn't plan it, but it is obvious with hindsight that I felt the need to start this movement for siblings in order to provide them with the early connection that Andi and I did not have.

I moved quickly. I was not interested in business plans and financial forecasts. I didn't want to tell too many people, because that would undoubtedly invite too many opinions. I just envisioned a camp. Camps made memories. A camp where siblings could belong, thus Camp To Belong!

I wrote a short 'to-do' list. Firstly, I garnered a visit to Stuart Fredlund, the Director of Children and Family Services in Clark County. I knew his approval was critical to open communication with social workers and foster parents if they were to learn, understand and be willing to let sibling groups come to camp. I shared my vision with Stuart, touching on my story, the importance of siblings and the idea of camp. While I wanted to respect his time, I really didn't want to say too much because I didn't want all the questions – for surely I did not yet know the answers. I was making it up as I went along. He gave me the go-ahead to bring siblings together.

Next, I needed volunteers to help turn the vision into reality. I reached out to a group of people with whom I had just completed CASA (Court Appointed Special Advocate) training, and urged them to participate in my vision. They responded positively and asked to be signed up with several close friends – even though we didn't know quite yet what they were signing up for. We were selective about who we told, because we knew the naysayers would suggest that an independent group could not provide overnight care for children and youth within the summer camp system.

We realised that we needed official documentation to bring credibility to the group and enable it to raise funds. I asked several close friends to be on the non-profit board. In amazement, but without hesitation, they agreed. In fact, my friend who had trouble balancing a cheque book became the treasurer. It was passion I was looking for.

While some naysayers said it would take a long time and cost a lot of money to fill out the paperwork to become a non-profit, our ardent supporters made it happen incredibly quickly. We became a 501c3 (a US non-profit) in record time and raised money through friends and community members and a kick-a-thon newly created by the martial arts studio where my own children and I practiced. We simply asked and people thought of their own siblings and responded.

We were checking off items on the to-do list, and the next project was the campsite. Camp environments are hard to come by in Las Vegas, so we visited the University of Las Vegas (UNLV), which was happy to offer its campus to our siblings in the summertime when students were on vacation. The negotiation was swift and affordable as they embraced our cause and decreased their rates.

That left the siblings. The volunteers, the board and I started pounding the pavement and communicating with members of our CASA cases, social workers, judges and shelter parents. Before we knew it, we had thirty-two brothers and sisters from seven to seventeen years old registered to come to camp.

So, three months from the vision date we held our first camp. Yes, just three months later! The more quickly we worked and looked as though we knew what we were doing, the faster siblings would connect.

Thirty-two brothers and sisters who were separated by foster care entered the dorm lobby at UNLV to the cheers of fifty-plus volunteer counsellors and project team members. Andi and I stood side by side, personifying the sibling possibilities on offer, including the opportunity to share a bedroom for the first time at camp.

Our first attempt at a camp schedule for six nights and seven days included many camp experiences to share between brothers and sisters, who put on their camp t-shirts and stared in awe. They were a bit tentative. After all, some were upset with a sibling who may have called the police about the trouble in the home. Or some had different fathers, which meant one may have had a different relative to go to. And, certainly, they wondered what all the adults were cheering about. Was it a trick to evaluate the camper's behaviour or feelings?

Our location was the University of Las Vegas. Not exactly the typical camp environment, especially when it was time for our opening campfire. Surrounded by buildings and cement, with no place for open fires in the 100+ degree heat, we met in the dorm room study hall, circled around the stacked logs, with the simulated flames of gold crepe paper spread out between them and glaring flashlights underneath, and ate our non-roasted campfire fare.

*Camp To Belong Nevada volunteer family ready to give siblings memories to last a lifetime. Photo courtesy of Camp To Belong Nevada.*

During the week we had laughter and tears. Silly camp songs. Fighting about who was going to sit next to who in the dining hall. Cheering each other on at recreational events. There was anxiety and opportunity as walls between campers came down and new friendships formed among them as they realised they were not alone in their challenges. The campers couldn't believe that the volunteers weren't paid to be there and swiftly accepted their care and mentoring. Some of the favourite memories were of siblings getting stuck in dorm room elevators or sharing a simple conversation as they laid their heads to rest.

*'You don't feel out of place because everyone around you is exactly like you. They're in exactly the same place as you ... and you feel like you belong.'* — Viktoriya

We improvised a variety of fun activities each day. Having learned that we could not use the university pool, we called the fire department

140

and the trucks showed up and showered our campers with water. It was too hot to go horseback riding, so the horses from the Excalibur Hotel Medieval Show came over and visited with a grooming clinic. The local physical education teacher came by to run a softball game of competition and cheerleading and the local art teacher crafted a poignant project for the siblings to share their feelings about each other through special scrolls.

*Siblings high five as they help each other to the top of the climbing wall. Photo courtesy of Camp To Belong Georgia/Teresa DeBroux.*

What we didn't expect was that the safe and comfortable environment for the campers allowed them to be themselves and freed them from the constraints of the system. The university was actually a conduit for them to learn that they have privileges as youths in care to attend college and be anything they want to be. Campers who had been forced to take on the role of parent at home, and whose own parents were unable to take care of them, had the chance to be children. The biggest bullies became the greatest leaders. The quiet and shy became the singers in the talent show. Brothers and sisters high-fived. Volunteers stretched the limits of their understanding in order to comprehend the challenges that these resilient kids faced through no fault of their own.

As we said goodbye to our campers on the final day, we celebrated the fact that each camper left Camp To Belong with a feeling of belonging, both to their sibling group and to the Camp To Belong family. I could only think: 'We just fell in love with thirty-two kids. They are filled up, as we are, and now what?' I didn't have a plan.

The 'now what', and the plan that ensued, took the form of a quest to Give Siblings Their Right to Reunite™ through ten more Camp To Belong summer camps around the USA and Australia, using a member camp business model that provides the basis for establishing further camps and training prospective providers.

The founding group of volunteers who stood behind, in front of and alongside the vision to bring significance to the sibling bond knew that replicating the programme on a larger scale was inevitable. The Camp To Belong member camps in Nevada, Orange County, California, Washington State, Oregon, Georgia, Maine, Massachusetts, New York, Colorado and Australia now welcome siblings separated by foster care, adoption and other out of home placement, providing them with the kind of experience offered by professional, residential, overnight camps. There are campfire pits, pools, lakes and oceans, stables, many sports activities and arts and crafts ... and no elevators!

Partnerships were established as like-minded organisations approached us, or we approached them, in each community of interest, to brainstorm how Camp To Belong could be an integrated service that enhanced the lives of siblings in the system. We were adamant about the need for unselfish collaboration. The volunteers are a mosaic of social workers who look at their jobs so differently now, including individuals from all walks of life – engineers, teachers, advertising geniuses, non-profit aficionados, and more.

The programmes promote the sibling connection among those experiencing the heartache of the foster care label and the separation between siblings. Campers are free to be themselves without the worry of what different sets of parents, social workers or therapists are going to say or think. Campers go home with shared camp memories, knowing that they'd established a sibling connection that would endure throughout the year.

*'Camp has changed my life. Miracles happen here.'* — *Andrew*

Many of the Camp To Belong member camps have started year-round reunions. Child welfare professionals are starting to look beyond the relationship between parent and child, and consider the impact of sibling separation, especially since the children are probably brought closer together by their shared exposure to parental strife.

It hasn't been easy. After the first camp, people asked a lot of questions. Mr Fredlund chuckled as he remarked that so many people come to him with ideas and don't implement them. Now that I had made it happen, he needed to know more.

Scaling up cannot happen quickly. It requires careful thought, and time to evaluate intention and protect a brand. As we expanded to our first multi-state camp, which was a result of my family move from Las Vegas to Denver, we needed to navigate through the challenges of bringing youths in foster care across state lines. The first camp brought forty campers from Nevada to Colorado, by plane, as we convinced the professionals that the Rocky Mountains made a more suitable camp location than a college campus. Bringing campers from the two states together led to increased awareness about the phenomenon of sibling separation, especially when a genuinely caring journalist with Parade Magazine told our story.

Attention shifted and resources abounded as volunteers contacted us nationwide, foster families pleaded for youths in their care to be allowed to spend time with their siblings, child welfare organisations accepted the 'help' to enhance sibling connection and our mighty team kept believing we could make Camp To Belong better and better as a place for fun, sibling connection and emotional empowerment.

*'For the past several years I have felt lost without my siblings. Now I feel found and that I have a purpose for being here. My siblings.' — Lucy*

We had to transform what was an innovative idea into something that could be replicated more widely. One year we flew in eighty campers to join those from Colorado, along with volunteers from other states who were keen to study our model.

Manuals had to be compiled to protect the integrity of the programmes, and fundraising was required to cover the cost of siblings flying from as far afield as Canada, the US Virgin Islands, Oregon and New Mexico.

The volunteer pool grew as we realised that we needed the organisational skills of year-round planners alongside the enthusiasm of those budding counsellors and those who wanted to jump in the trenches with the youths, as well as the exceptional residential camp teams who opened their doors to us pre- or post-season. We needed to tighten up the training.

The activities began to take on more meaning. We organised inspirational forums. Siblings created pillows to present to each other and bring to their respective homes. They filled scrapbooks with the only pictures they have had of their siblings. They took part in a carnival where they shared the joys of dunk tanks and snow cones, and even a birthday party where they gave each other presents and blew out the candles on their shared birthday cakes. Each activity afforded them the opportunity to learn about each other again. And with a life

*Sisters Lynn (right) and Andi (left) as Camp Carnival Clowns. Photo courtesy of Ed Andrieski.*

seminar for the older siblings and community service project for the younger siblings (the only activities undertaken in different groups) they learned not to be a victim of circumstances, but to be a victor. Like Andi and me, they learned how not to become just another statistic, like so many youths in care who end up spending their adult lives in prison, homeless and un-educated. Like us, they could be college grads, and have families and careers.

The most difficult thing for me was running a passion alongside a business. The most important catalyst for growth was sharing the vision with others who believed and dedicated their time and expertise. Where I just wanted to make things happen, they would offer perspective and force me to focus on reality and process. When I wanted to plan something before the money was raised, adopting a 'build it and they will come' attitude, my wonderful, honest comrades would bring me back down to earth. And as Camp To Belong grew, it was paramount to run the venture like a business, which nevertheless involved putting people in place who would embrace the passion and protect the vision.

The amazing thing about embracing a vision is that you need to be opportunistic and spontaneous. You may make a decision because it just feels right, without any research and based on pure instinct.

My vision was broad, but in short windows. I planned the first camp with a merry band of friends and then we thought about the 'what happens next'. Year-round programmes and camps across the USA and abroad were ready to learn from us. We created a member camp model to scale up the brand. Legislation regarding sibling placement and visitation emerged alongside sibling bills of rights. Recruitment of more foster and adoptive families for siblings increased. Tight-knit sibling groups started looking at their own relationships in different ways and some brothers and sisters who had consciously separated due to sibling rivalry started to reconnect.

Fundraising is a challenge for most organisations, and ours was no exception. There is a myth that 'just' having a one-week camp for a limited amount of time with a small group of campers does not have an impact. Believe all of us, it makes an impact that lasts a whole lifetime, as we educate all year round and create indelible memories. We like to approach contributors with the request to think of their own siblings, their children, or their best friend who is like a sibling, and to imagine life without them. Most cannot, and are therefore willing to contribute in any way they can.

The greatest advice I can give an emerging social entrepreneur is to be solution-oriented. To revolutionise and to create a new definition of state-of-the-art for something that is meaningful to them and about which they are passionate:

- Stop talking and just do it. Take ownership of an *innovation*, an out-of-this-world (but maybe common-sense) vision. Doing it creates your own laboratory where business models then thrive in reality.
- Use your *entrepreneurial* skills with gut instinct, taking risks and improvising along the way to maximise the possibilities.

- Take on the naysayers. After all, 'never been done' does not mean 'cannot be done.'
- Share your contagious energy *creatively*. I call it the 'power of the ripple'. Cast that one stone across that still pond and watch the waves spread out as you change the world, and invite and embrace others who believe alongside you.
- Don't reinvent the wheel. Learn from others and accept that you don't know everything, and invite others to offer their expertise.
- Be complimented by the competition, or those who actually copy. Keep your guard down, subjugate your ego and unselfishly ask them to collaborate.
- Don't race once you leave the starting gate. Everything is on schedule.
- Give the benefit of the doubt to the possibility that there is a method to the madness that may not make sense to others, but is crystal clear to you.
- Be ready for whatever materialises, for the *impact* you don't expect.
- Make sure that your organisation has the right combination of passion and business nous. Replicate with intention and *integrity*.

## ACKNOWLEDGEMENTS

Thank you to my sister, Andi, for the encouragement. When I told you about my vision for Camp To Belong, you said you never heard of anything like a camp for siblings separated by foster care, but if anyone could do it, it would be me! Thanks to my children, Addison, Tanner, Jamie, Bryan, Jenny and Zach, for unselfishly sharing your lives with all the kids who come through our doors at home, and at Camp To Belong. Thanks to all those advocates, volunteers, care providing teams, partners, board, staff, contributors and campers for believing in the quest to 'give siblings their right to reunite'. Together, we are the 'power of the ripple'!

# 8

# PATENT WARS

## Priti Radhakrishnan

*An unexpected conversation over dinner leads to the
birth of an innovative new organisation with
a mission to fight for the rights of people
denied access to life-saving medicines.*

A stranger's heartbreak can be unforgettable. As I prepared for a
client meeting with Rahim – his name is changed here for confi-
dentiality reasons – I had no idea my life was about to change. I was
working in India as the project manager of a legal aid organisation that
represented and advocated for indigent HIV-positive clients, and I frequently encountered clients who could not afford anti-retroviral therapy or medications for opportunistic infection.

Rahim stood out, though. At seventeen he was so severely malnour-
ished that he looked no more than seven. He was sweet, articulate and
desperately fighting to continue his education, despite his illness. The
recipient of a negligent blood transfusion at a government hospital in

147

Tamil Nadu, India, HIV had ravaged his delicate frame. As I prepared to file his petition in court to seek damages and free medication, I realised something had changed within me. After five years as an attorney, I was no longer satisfied to only advocate at the local level for impoverished patients and communities. I needed to change the systems that were standing in the way of getting treatment to all patients. I needed to bring together experts that could take on a market that was failing communities – communities whose immunologic failure could be reversed.

This is how my journey to build I-MAK began.

## THE BEGINNING

In truth, my journey began when I was seven. My Delhi-based grandfather gave me a dictionary, and these words from the Pakistani poet Faiz: 'I shall place a tongue in every link of chain that fetters me.' My grandfather was a pioneer of the working journalists' movement and a freedom fighter in Gandhi's struggle for independence. He explained to me that while he was imprisoned in Alipuram Jail, he started an underground newspaper written on slates, dreaming of a better tomorrow for the dispossessed. In that moment, my grandfather gave me a precious gift. He showed me that words are a weapon, to be used with skill and for peace.

He altered the course of my life with that gift – along with the rest of our family. I grew up thinking it was ordinary to have a family for whom the ability to hold, house and uplift an entire community was not a righteous aspiration, but a calling.

I am born from this blood.

I needed to go back to the place where they did their *seva*, or service, to understand the communities that made up my family's country. I now realise that my family is anything but ordinary: a collective of organisers, scientists, teachers and journalists in which fierce political discussions around the dinner table were the norm. I needed to go back so I could learn how to do my own *seva*, with more depth and precision and understanding, and not from a comfortable law firm office in Los Angeles or from a prestigious desk in Geneva.

I needed to sit with communities day in and day out, year after year, to learn first-hand the struggles they endured, without prescription or any assumption that I could possibly understand what needed to be done. And after sitting quietly for some time, perhaps I could begin to roll up my sleeves and take on the tasks they felt needed to be done.

I walked into a travel agency and bought a one-way ticket to Delhi.

# THE INDIA YEARS

In 2003, I joined the relentless human rights non-governmental organisation, the Lawyers Collective, which advocated for communities affected by HIV, pushing the Indian government to introduce a free treatment programme. I helped co-ordinate these efforts nationally. India expanded its free treatment programme, and patients such as Rahim underwent dramatic transformations in their health. Through this journey, I witnessed first-hand the power and direct effects of advocacy on behalf of those who could not give voice to their lack of access to health services and treatment.

### The movement to shape India's new patent law.
The biggest fight loomed ahead. India, which supplied affordable medicines to most of the developing world, had reached a crossroads. It had committed to introducing a patent law that would provide ownership rights to pharmaceutical companies, a new and troubling direction for the country.

This was an ominous policy reversal. India had a long history of progressive action on affordable medicines. After ousting the British in 1947, India realised it had some of the highest medicine prices in the world, and set up a committee to investigate whether this hangover of colonial rule – the patent law – was meeting its society's needs. After finding that most patent holders were foreign companies, India made a courageous move. In 1972 the country decided to abolish its patent law, allowing for the emergence of a domestic industry that could supply its citizenry.

Over the next twenty-five years, India became a self-sufficient country. Without foreign companies holding monopoly rights on medicines, India was able to grow its own drug industry, and provide its citizens with more affordable drugs. Importantly, India's drug industry started supplying the developing world. It became the world's 'pharmacy for the poor.' India went from having the highest prices to the lowest prices, all by removing its patent law and promoting its own drug industry.

And in 2001, in a move that would shape the course of my own life, India broke the dominant paradigm. At a moment when Western pharmaceutical companies claimed they could not bring annual HIV drug prices below $10,000 per patient, the Indian generic industry said it would provide the medicines for less than a tenth of that cost. From that moment, India became the supplier of low-cost HIV medicines to the Global South.

But then India joined the World Trade Organisation (WTO), setting in motion a series of events that led to the weakening of its own industry by providing ownership rights to pharmaceutical companies. With a new WTO-backed patent law on the way – likely to destroy the domestic generics industry – the need for action was urgent. In neighbouring countries, drug prices had surged as high as 700%. And in India, drug prices began to rise after the government signalled its willingness to become a part of the international trading system.

*Indian protest around the patent bill. Photo courtesy of Tahir Amin.*

Everyone at the Lawyers Collective got to work. For two years I visited villages across rural and urban India, working with my team to organise, educate and advocate with community members. The subject matter – patent law – was complex, but community activists who lived with HIV and cancer were able to make the issues clear to everyday people. From garment workers to sex workers, from farmers to day labourers, people realised the severity of what was happening. Together these groups mobilised, organised and came together in conjunction with treatment activists from around the world. Protests took place from Delhi to Nairobi, from Bangkok to Rio, to New York and Johannesburg.

## Sleepless nights: the passage of the Indian Patent(s) Act, 2005.
After months of organising the moment came when we least expected it.

In March 2005, the Lawyers Collective convened a meeting in Mumbai with people living with HIV and leading treatment activists from all over the Global South – Brazil, China, Sri Lanka, South Africa, Thailand and more. Our plan was to spend three days envisioning the road ahead for the global movement.

But that conversation never happened. By sheer coincidence, on the very day the leading voices of the treatment activist movement landed in Mumbai, the Indian Parliament began debating the patent bill which was set to provide *unfettered* ownership rights to the multinational pharmaceutical industry. In other words, there were insufficient public health safeguards in the bill to ensure access to affordable medicines. I have never been a big believer in destiny, but there is no other word to describe this moment.

Our coalition jumped to action to stop the bill from passing without public health safeguards. We organised a press conference featuring activists from around the world who had spent years of their lives fighting for access to medicines. The South Africans led us in a song that railed against HIV skepticism. The Indians led us in protest chants from the Indian labour and independence movement. And the head of the Indian Cancer Patients Aid Association spoke with a trembling voice about the plight of low-income cancer patients unable to access life-saving medication.

The next morning we flew from Mumbai to Delhi, where we worked day and night for nearly a week to lobby Parliament to reject a patent law that did not include public health protections. I will never forget sitting in that office, crammed with activists from all over the world, calling up Indian Members of Parliament at 2am to demand they listen to our communities and stop the bill that was set to pass at sunrise. We chased down parliamentarians at their homes, did media interviews and wrote article after article.

Hours later we heard that the bill had passed, *with* public health safeguards. Communities alone could not have won this battle, and the generic companies alone could not have prevailed. This victory spoke to the power of the treatment activist movement from around the world, which mobilised to ensure that access could be a reality.

India took a tremendous step as a leader in the developing world to ensure that the new patent system would not override the public health of its citizens, or decimate the domestic generic drug industry. The law created an open and democratic system that allowed for a 'citizen review' in which anyone could register opposition to a patent. And it required pharmaceutical companies that were re-tweaking older compounds to show actual therapeutic benefit for patients. This was an unprecedented move by India, the first of any country to make a patient-centered demand of pharmaceutical companies. The global trade balances had tilted in favour of the voiceless.

## OUR FIRST PATENT CASE

The thing that still surprises me even after all these years is that we won the battle and got health safeguards into the patent law. We won. Any activist will tell you that victories such as this are few and far between. When they come, we savour them. Often, we use that victory as fuel for years, to remind us that we are not simply fighting in the face of futility.

Shortly after the patent law passed, while still working at the Lawyers Collective, I created a unit to engage in citizen review of patents using the newly enacted health safeguard. Our intention was to ensure that unlawful patents would not be granted, particularly those that could block access to affordable medicines. In that capacity, our team filed the first citizen intervention using the newly enacted patent law in India. Remarkably, we moved from protests on the street to technocratic fights at the patent office.

Our first case was filed on behalf of an organisation providing lifesaving drugs to low-income cancer patients at little or no cost. The Swiss company Novartis had obtained an exclusive right in India to an important leukemia drug. The price of Gleevec, a drug for chronic myeloid leukemia, had skyrocketed to $2,600 a month from $200. In a country where the majority of citizens live on less than $2 a day, where there is no comprehensive insurance system nor any broad social safety net, these cancer patients could not afford this drug even if their lives depended on it, which they did.

Over the next year we pursued our case against Novartis with advocacy, using the legal system in an unprecedented way and registering our resistance to a new global trade regime that threatened the rights of low-income patients. To support the opposition, my team met with communities in a series of town hall meetings across India, explaining the legal nuances and organising media briefings. And in fighting the case, we helped create a new movement of political resistance against unfettered private rights across the developing world. Our victory in shaping the patent law was giving birth to a whole new wave of activism.

## STARTING A NEW ORGANISATION

Around this time, I was living with a close friend and her husband in Bangalore. They were a married couple from California, and one night over dinner after I returned home from a town hall meeting we stayed up late into the night talking. I was irate about the price of the Novartis leukemia drug in India, and distressed at how low-income patients would access the drug until the case was resolved, if an injunction against generics was issued. My friends asked if I had thought about starting my own organisation to address this problem on a global scale. I said I hadn't, and they asked what it would cost to get it off the ground. When I responded that I had no idea, they told me they wanted to write me a cheque for $200,000 to see what I could get done.

In retrospect, I marvel at my luck. It is the dream of most entrepreneurs to have such friends, and such a moment. We did not know it at the time, but a year later my friend's husband would be diagnosed with cancer. He would go on to beat it back home in California. And his and their generosity would ensure that other patients without access to medicines would have an opportunity to do the same.

**Making the decision.**

My work on the Gleevec case made me realise I could no longer serve as a community organiser and advocate. India's new patent law created a need for lawyers to take on the multinational pharmaceutical industry and the systems that propped up the industry – on their own turf. And the work had to be done not only in India, which served as the supplier to most other developing countries, but also in those recipient countries. Unless we removed patents in low- and middle-income countries as a parallel effort to our Indian opposition, access would be obstructed. There was a need for a global public interest group with top-notch intellectual property and pharmaceutical sciences expertise to represent the interests of low-income patients around the world.

And so I could no longer do the work that, quite simply, made me come alive – working with people living with diseases within their communities, addressing their immediate legal and advocacy needs. I was needed elsewhere, to help create a team of highly skilled and nimble lawyers and scientists who could help stop the seemingly unstoppable pharmaceutical industry.

However, I shuddered at the thought of managerial responsibility and administrative work, of leaving my communities in India to work globally. The thought of focusing exclusively on patents instead of working comprehensively on access issues terrified me. In fact, I could not think of anything less interesting than working on patent issues from a desk in New York when I would much prefer to be engaging daily with the Indian institutions and individuals obstructing access for my clients, and taking action locally. If anyone was ever reluctant, it was me.

At the time I didn't pause to stop and think about the decision. The long road to becoming a human rights lawyer and community organiser enabled me to profoundly understand the commitment that I was about to make in starting down a new path – one that would be longer and more intensive than anything I had ever experienced. I was prepared for those challenges. For me this was no longer a choice. I was compelled by my experiences to make this commitment to the communities I had worked and fought alongside. And, with the generous offer of my friends, I had the ability to make that commitment a reality.

**The early days.**
In the early days of I-MAK, we – three co-founders, interns and consultants – huddled around my dining table working on cases late into the night. We hopped on planes and filed cases in the patent offices of Kolkata, Chennai, Mumbai and Delhi, building relationships with patent examiners and learning the system from the inside out.

Those were lonely days. Other NGOs shunned us as they felt that our intervention could have been built into one of their existing organisations. We felt they did not understand the necessity for a new organisation, one that could be nimble and responsive, that would not face bureaucratic hurdles and bottlenecks. Where they saw insult, we saw opportunity, and it took many years for us to repair the relationships that grew strained during that time.

But we plodded on, confident in our vision. We filed case after case, built our team of lawyers and scientists, raised money, built our board, and put up a website. Step by step, I-MAK came into its own. I can recall taking sixty flights a year in those early years, speaking publicly, attending conferences, visiting patent offices and communities without access across the developing world. I was on the road to building a lasting organisation, but I was also walking down a path to burnout. I just didn't know it yet.

**Unexpected struggles.**
My story is incomplete without details of the political context of this period, and my personal struggles that came about as a result.

In July 2006, with I-MAK still in its infancy, my soon-to-be-husband and activist partner was a target of racial profiling. As a Muslim of Pakistani-British descent, he had the misfortune of flying from

Mumbai to London the week of the Mumbai bomb blasts of 11th July, 2006. He had finished giving a talk for generic companies, and stepped onto the plane, thinking of nothing but work, visiting his aging parents in London and coming back to India to be with me. But he never made it. At the Indian Consulate in the United Kingdom, he was denied a visa back to India without explanation. I will never forget the moment when the police arrived at my Bangalore apartment to investigate him, when they tapped his Indian mobile phone, or when I opened his closet, and, painstakingly and with an ache in my heart, packed his clothes into one suitcase after another.

One injustice compounded another. For a year we lived apart, yet continued our work to ensure access to medicines, and took care of our relationship by meeting in Brazil, South Africa and numerous parts of the United States and the UK. But the political fallout against Muslims in the post-9/11 world had changed everything. In our visits to the US and UK I sat waiting as my partner was taken away for 'secondary inspection' or selected for a 'random security check', often spending uncertain hours in anguish wondering whether I would see him again, or whether we would be allowed to enter the country. We wanted, badly, to be angry, hurt. Instead, we learned to practice compassion and forgiveness.

In late 2006, I received an e-mail in Delhi that altered my life forever. My 'little brother', Vinay, had leukemia. Without hesitation I packed up my belongings and moved to Boston. My entire life shifted in focus, both to the United States and to a new role. I became his caregiver: nurturing, sustaining, healing. Vinay needed a bone-marrow transplant and there weren't enough minority donors for him – or other patients – to find a match. So I started a bone marrow donor campaign. We beat every record: 25,000 minority donors in eight weeks. Sheltered by our community's strength, we cared for thousands.

Against the backdrop of these challenges, my work had to continue. I worked from Vinay's room at the Dana-Farber Cancer Institute, and was blessed to have guardian angels such as Jim Kim, who ensured I had a space to work at the Harvard School of Public Health. At every critical step of the journey I had benefactors who helped me and ensured that the work could continue. From these rooms in Boston,

I-MAK filed one of our most important patent challenges, against a company called Abbott Laboratories, to increase affordable access to the HIV drug Kaletra.

In early 2008, my childhood best friend, Priya, died of a sudden neurological complication. We sang to Priya's body as she slipped away. Then, Vinay succumbed to his leukemia. Organising two funerals two months apart, and reciting prayers for parents saying goodbye to their children, are fates I wouldn't wish upon anyone.

*'Om purnamadah purnamidam … when fullness is taken away, fullness still remains.'*

In the months that followed, I allowed myself to completely absorb the loss. The years of working 100-hour weeks in India, of constant travel to rural villages and visits across the urban centers of many countries in the Global South, had caught up with me. In my deepest grief I recognised that losing my dearest friends was compounded by years of working with people living with serious diseases. I watched children being taken away to orphanages and ashrams as their parents succumbed to opportunistic infection, and parents holding their dying children because HIV treatment was unavailable. Seeing these moments year after year had broken my spirit. To lose friends I had known longer than any other made life feel unbearable. At thirty I turned away from my work, feeling a visceral rejection of any mention of access to medicines from the open wound inside of me.

**Healing.**

During the following year, 2009, I made a daily choice to not yield to the traumatic stress that threatened to engulf me. I went inward and I went deep. I danced, cooked, practiced yoga, cried, knit, laughed, planted and taught pilates. Pilates, an approach to mind-body movement, would ground me in the years to come. I learned to nurture myself with the same intensity and gentle touch I gave to others. This descendant of a Gandhian family had to learn that *seva*, or service, must be practiced through non-duality: there is no difference between you and others. Loving kindness must be imparted to all, equally. Even in the face of tragedy. Even to your own self.

And through this journey, I learned to let go of my work. No longer did I have the desire or the drive to bulldoze through my caseload, endure sleepless nights or fight with gentle ferocity to make changes within a system that imposed seemingly endless structural resistance. With a heavy heart, and a significant amount of guilt, I let go, gently, of my work. I slowed down significantly, only taking on what I could accomplish without my heart. It made me feel less alive, but looking back it gave me the space I needed to heal and move forward. It is one of the hardest lessons I have learned and it needed me to completely crumple in order for it to happen.

**Another loss.**
*On this new path of seva, I learned to meditate through the layers of dizzying loss, and sit with my satya, or truth.*

*Loss changes you, it goes to the very tensegrity of the structures that comprise you and it erodes and remakes them. My husband and I, we were different now.*

*Forgiving myself for changing was the hardest step of my journey. It taught me how to move halfway into my asana, upside down and in between, how to breathe into the unknown. It compelled me to just be, to accept what is real.*

*And once self-forgiveness came, the rest fell into place. With grace, love and honesty, I said goodbye to the man who had danced in my heart for nearly a decade.*

*There is an agony and a joy that unfolds when we tap into the courage we never knew lived within us, a wholeness that emerges when we are strong enough to listen to the voice that resides in the shadows of that temple within.*

*The voice says, 'fly'.*
*I'm soaring now...*

**Finding my way back.**
After nearly three years tending to the work of my soul, I acknowledged that my relationship to my work was now different. I accepted my detachment from the subject matter, although I continued to feel wistful about the impact that my loss of passion would have on

communities I worked with. I viewed the shift within me with the finality that young people do when they don't know any better, when they don't know that life keeps changing and that, with it, you will, too. I looked at my days as a fiery treatment activist as a relic of the past, with a mixture of bittersweet relief and guilt. But then, as they do, things changed again.

Sometimes it doesn't take a life-altering moment to bring you back. After walking on a very dark road for a very long time with nothing to illuminate my path, I had learned to just place one foot in front of the other, find steady ground, and to keep on moving. And then one day, just like that, I walked myself into the light. I just stepped into my old-new self and found an energy. I'll never understand how it happened, but maybe I don't need to. What matters is that I never formally left I-MAK during those years. My organisation, my co-founder, my board and everyone around me were supportive of redesigning my role to meet my reality during those difficult days. For this I will be eternally grateful.

After I found my way back to my work, I discovered a new energy to advocate on issues of access to treatment. As I-MAK expanded to new countries, to new diseases, I found myself engaged and inspired by my partners in middle-income countries, and delighted to discover my old skills of excavating information and strategically intervening to support communities in their quest to increase access to medicines.

The truth, for me, is that burnout happened in part because in my line of work I was never going to meet the vast majority of people I have helped. There was no energy coming back my way to help restore and fuel me for the next round. On top of that, in the private sector, compensation or revenue help determine an individual or institution's worth. In the NGO sector, particularly in health, most of the value is derived from public profile. It is why even the best NGOs are drawn into the ego game, and it is why the lack of recognition or profile can start to affect people with the most noble of intentions. It took me years to recognise these realities and even longer to design a life that could nourish me and enable me to work effectively.

In the last year, I have finally dissolved the guilt that I carried for lessening my role in I-MAK. To others it sounds crazy that I would carry guilt when I cared for a cancer patient, ran a bone marrow campaign to help save a life, and recovered from the unexpected loss of my two best friends. But my commitment to treatment activism was so unwavering that I did not understand what I do now. We do a disservice to the work, and to the communities that we serve, when we give 300% of ourselves to it. That's a sure-fire recipe for burnout. It decides for us that we will not last over time. It depletes us long before it should.

Today, I work differently. I take pride in the fact that I have been a treatment activist for a decade, and that I-MAK is now in its seventh year of operation. But as I board a flight to Pakistan or South Africa or Argentina, I stop to buy a neck pillow. I mark off days in my calendar to recoup when I get back. I teach mindful movement three days a week in New York City, ensuring I have a practice that grounds me, that helps me remember the mind-body connection, and that balances my activism.

And this summer, when we were dealt a severe blow with the unanticipated death of a staff member, I paused to absorb the loss. Not only was he the driving force behind I-MAK's scientific work, he was a friend and a mentor as well. After years of dealing with loss, I felt unprepared for yet another goodbye. But this time was different, because I instinctively gave myself the space to absorb the shock, to grieve, to express the pain, to send love to his family, and months later to begin to rebuild our team. This time there was no guilt around the process and no self-forgiveness needed. I had finally learned that when life happens, resistance is futile.

## MORE LESSONS

In one of the critical turning points in my journey as an activist, I began to integrate a principle that my friend and activist Ai-Jen Poo taught me – to 'organise with love'. Most of us activists run on the fuel of passion, adrenaline or even anger at injustice. When you organise with love – engaging governments, companies and international institutions as partners instead of advocacy targets – a shift takes place. I found that I was no longer depleting myself of critical energy reserves. And that internal shift reflected itself externally as well. This new approach drove collaborative responses and moved debates that were previously entrenched in disagreement.

At the same time, I was thinking about real impact and how to design for it, and I realised that, for an activist, the ultimate expression of love is real, measurable change. As taught by impact expert Kevin Starr, there are two questions that matter the most: what are we trying to do, and do we know that it is working? I started to apply rigorous tools for impact measurement as a vital component of advocacy. I brought evidence-based insights into the field of access to treatment to show which strategies were and were not working and how they could be improved. As Gandhi famously said, '*Be the change that you wish to see in the world.*' Learning to understand and measure our impact, while organising with love, allowed us to be that change.

## VICTORY

After all of this learning and evolving, I had completely let go of any expectation of winning. Being a treatment activist means you learn how to fight against structural resistance month after month, year after year, with little expectation of conquering the system. I had survived on passion and adrenaline years ago when I filed important cases that I hoped might open the door for affordable medicines for the Global South. And, now, I had learned to work through the phases when my passion felt extinguished. But my mind rarely, if ever, wondered how the story would end.

In 2011, we won the case against Abbott Laboratories for that HIV drug, the one we first filed sitting in that hospital room in Boston. I remember the moment I heard the news. I was incredulous, filled with disbelief. It had taken four years for the decision to come down. That a few lawyers and scientists sitting on their laptops could take on a behemoth company with an army of lawyers and unlimited funds was improbable. Yet the Indian law itself gave us the opening, allowing for 'citizen review' of patents at little or no cost. All it took was a team of experts who cared enough to commit to the cause. In our first three cases alone, we estimated that more than 700,000 lives would be affected in the first five years. Margaret Mead's quote, which I had always believed to be true, came alive for me at this moment:

*'Never doubt that a small group of thoughtful, committed citizens can change the world. Indeed, it's the only thing that ever has.'*

This year, 2013, those words rang true again. Eight years after the first case against Novartis was filed, eight years of work by lawyers, activists and patients around the world, the Indian Supreme Court decided in favour of patients, the access to medicines movement and of India to preserve its right to enact health safeguards in the context of trade. The victory was groundbreaking. I sat in Chennai in stunned silence for nearly a day and absorbed what it meant to win with this leukaemia drug. The next day, the *New York Times* called to ask what I-MAK thought of the decision. Our response was swift and decisive. The ripple effects of this decision would be felt across the globe, and other low- and middle-income countries would follow India's lead. Beyond increased access to affordable versions of this leukemia drug, other countries including Argentina have now moved to protect public health within their patent regimes.

In the end, this victory took eight years to come to fruition. Eight long, lonely, tiring years of my own life, years where I wondered if our movement would ever make a dent in the uncompromising machinery of the pharmaceutical industry, or the systems that protect profits at the expense of human life. Eight agonising years of watching children say goodbye to their parents, and parents say goodbye far too early to their children. If this decade has taught me anything, it is that great change takes time, and patience is the cornerstone of *seva*.

And today my understanding of that *seva* is different. It is no longer a perception of giving wholly of oneself, of service at the expense of the self. I ensure that work-life balance exists, and I serve as a mentor to younger activists and entrepreneurs to help them shape their lives to best serve themselves, and to best serve their work. In the end, the lesson I learned on duality at a meditation retreat is the one I continually come back to, remembering I am not different or disconnected from the communities I seek to serve, or the world, which I believe are interconnected. So today, *seva* to myself is an integral part of my larger service.

**Integration.**

As I sit here today, writing these words, it amazes me how much has happened in the last decade. I imagine my grandfather, seeing me now, sitting at this small wood table, typing furiously, feeling proud because I am flourishing. The drive he instilled in me, the drive he possessed every working day of his life to give voice to marginalised communities, still propels me forward. His values of living simply, as a senior-level journalist until the end of his days, without a car or a telephone, are ones I share and constantly strive to emulate. I believe that if he could see I-MAK, now working across the world with communities in many countries, working on more diseases, with a growing team, I think he would be over the moon.

I look back on the last decade of my life and sometimes think that I wouldn't wish it on anyone. But the truth is, my hardships gave me this life. This great and sometimes overwhelming grief showed me parts of life that I may have been too caught up in to otherwise notice. In the end it was my very suffering that 'compelled me to reach'. And that's my (simple, complex, boundless) truth.

# 9

# WITHOUT MUD THERE IS NO LOTUS

## Sharon Terry

*Until a visit to the dermatologist turns her world upside down,
Sharon Terry has never heard of pseudoxanthoma elasticum
(PXE), but when she discovers that research into the disease
afflicting her children is hidebound by scientific protocol, she
sets about changing the system with characteristic zeal.*

### CROSSING THE THRESHOLD

There are those moments in life you know you will remember forever. They constitute a clear and delineated threshold. You cross it
and there is no going back. It is very different than remembering where
you were when you heard that John Kennedy was shot, or the Berlin
Wall was no longer a barrier. Life is a different colour and hue on the
other side.

This sort of moment propelled me into a reluctant, deeper, entrepreneurism. I say deeper, because it led to the discovery that I have been a reluctant entrepreneur all of my life. Adversities of one kind or another have called my creativity forth and refined it in a crucible, a process that I often fought against. For me, the essence of who I am has been called into fullness by adversity. Entrepreneurism is simply a mechanism, and sometimes the expression of a neurosis, by which I have become me.

The build-up to that moment was a particular kind of rollercoaster ride, sometimes called the diagnostic odyssey. I was at my niece's first birthday party in 1992, the first happy event since the death of my brother about four months before, and I noticed in the softening sunlight three small dots on each side of my daughter's neck. It was a hot September afternoon in Connecticut, and I thought about this discovery for a moment, feeling a little flip of fear in my stomach, and then let it go – returning to the quest for equilibrium for our extended family in the face of the large hole left by Stephen's death at thirty-one years old.

*Elizabeth and Ian Terry at the time of their diagnosis. Photo by author.*

Over the next months, and years, I asked our paediatrician periodically: 'What are these dots? Why are they only on the sides of her neck? Why are they slowly increasing in number over time? Are they important? Should I ignore them?' She repeatedly reassured me that I was needlessly worried. She suggested it was a laundry detergent allergy. I wasn't convinced and silently baulked – why weren't these dots all the way around her neck? Then, reassuring myself, I would agree with her that I was neurotically suspicious of the slightest thing since my brother's death, and yes, I should be in therapy mitigating that neurosis. Or probably these dots weren't really progressing, right? Then why did photos from year to year look so different? Thank goodness I was in therapy as this chapter unfolded!

I do not know what finally led us to it, but my husband Pat and I decided to go 'out-of-pocket' and 'out-of-plan' to a dermatologist – meaning we would pay for the visit to a physician that wasn't approved by our particular insurance plan. I set up an appointment, told Pat he needn't come since I would undoubtedly hear that it was an allergy of some sort, and off we went, Elizabeth and her younger brother Ian, to see the doctor on December 23rd, 1994 – that defining moment looming up ahead as we marched into it, oblivious.

It all happened in what seemed like a split second. Dr Lionel Bercovitch glanced at Elizabeth's neck, said 'She has pseudoxanthoma elasticum.' As my stomach began to churn at the sound of the syllable 'oma' (weren't there cancers like melanoma, and lymphoma?), he glanced at Ian and added, 'Oh, and he has it too.' Then he shut off the lights and looked in her eyes with an ophthalmoscope. 'What? Just stop right here!' I wanted to scream. This was a skin problem – what was he doing looking in her eyes? Yes, her eyes were affected too. I had crossed the threshold. I did not know where I was, I was frightened and it was dark.

Dr Bercovitch turned the lights back on, explained to me that he was trained in dermatology and ophthalmology and so could see both the skin and eye effects of pseudoxanthoma elasticum (PXE). I could not absorb the words he was speaking. Something about this being systemic, and an autosomal recessive disease, and not much being known about it. I just saw my gorgeous children, and heard him speak about wrinkly sagging skin and blindness.

I went home, called Pat and sobbed about the disfigurement that our children would be facing in their future. Oh, how foolish to worry about their skin and appearance, when blindness was a strong possibility! I then called our paediatrician. She pulled a book from her shelves and read to me. This was a disease that would cause skin, eye, cardiac and vascular problems. Pat came home and we tried to have a normal dinner so the kids wouldn't worry, too.

Dr Bercovitch called us after dinner. We thought this extraordinary, but were even more astounded to learn that he lived just a few houses away. He offered to speak with us the next evening, Christmas Eve, at his house, while another neighbour came and watched Elizabeth and

Ian. That night, we struggled to understand what he was telling us and realised we knew too little to digest it. We would need some basic references and then some time to get up to speed.

Elizabeth and Ian remember that Christmas, when they were seven and five years old respectively, as the best Christmas of their lives. They got every toy they wished for and more. They were joyful and happy little kids, unaware that anything had changed. As they learned about the condition, they learned the long Latin name. They began to name spiders and plants 'Pseudoxanthoma elasticum' – believing it sounded sufficiently scientific.

## Discovering the Problem Is Beyond Us

The weeks following Christmas were difficult ones. I went to two medical school libraries and photocopied every article on PXE that I could find, pawing through the card catalogue in those pre-Internet days. I brought home 400 articles, and couldn't understand any of them – only that there were grotesque photos of sagging skin, and descriptions of early blindness and premature death. Pat and I eagerly and anxiously combed through the articles, and though we were clueless as to the details, we began to see patterns.

The first pattern: there was no pattern. These authors were writing from a hundred different perspectives, only reporting one case, and then drawing conclusions about the disease from the single case. We did not understand how one could characterise a disease with only one case, something we later learned is called an 'N of 1'. The next pattern that was apparent to us was that seemingly unrelated things were associated and supposed to tell a story. As an example, there was a paper on a 13-year-old who died 'from PXE'. However, she also had a seizure disorder and had attempted suicide several times. We couldn't tell whether PXE was the cause of her death. How could the author be certain? Who were we to question the author of a scientific paper, published in a journal?

PXE appeared to be characterised differently in different geographic locations, and while it is certainly true that geographic isolation or ancestral origin could produce variations in the disease, there seemed to be extreme differences between similar populations. It was also troubling that all of the reports were positive – there were no failed experiments reported. How would researchers learn if the failed experiments were not made public? Another pattern that emerged was a lack of collaboration. In the few cases where an author wrote multiple papers, it seemed that those papers were with the same group of authors. There was no cross-over, or cross-fertilisation.

The issue of collaboration, or actually competition, became poignantly clear for us in the days following the diagnosis of our children. A few days after Christmas, a scientist from Harvard called to ask whether he could have a sample of our children's blood for a study seeking to find the gene associated with PXE. We readily agreed to the visit from the researcher's assistant and the kids' blood was drawn. Two days later a researcher from Mt Sinai Hospital called and asked the same. We told him: 'Sure, the researcher from Harvard took several vials and certainly he would share. No one would ask little children to have blood drawn twice!' He chuckled: 'No, they won't share with us, we are racing each other to find the gene.' This was astounding to us. While of course we had seen competition in many areas of life, it was unthinkable that there was competition in biomedical research. Wasn't everyone focused on solving these issues as soon as possible, with the highest degree of collaboration since the stakes were huge? No, that is not what was happening. We were shocked.

Another pattern that emerged is that nothing was being done systematically about this disease. There was no learning from one paper to another, experiments were repeated, and no one was mapping the scientific patterns that might be found in the data. And finally, a strange and horrible pattern became evident. People were called subjects in these papers. They were not collaborators, and certainly not empowered to participate.

Within a month of Elizabeth's and Ian's diagnoses, we had to let go of the misconception that every disease had some treatment. We needed to step away from the illusion that this was the medical equivalent of a delicatessen counter. No one was going to call our number, so there was no use waiting hopefully until someone got to the 'P's. We also had to figure out a way to make order out of the chaos that appeared in the papers we read, and in the competition we experienced in the blood collections for research.

## SCIENCE: IS IT SO DIFFERENT FROM ALL OF THE OTHER CHALLENGES?

Trained as a teacher and a college chaplain, I was ill-prepared for the piles of medical journal papers. I was as clueless about research as my engineering husband, who is fond of saying 'we didn't know a gene from a hubcap'. It was not obvious to us or to those around us that we had it in us to change the system. But we had no choice.

As we fell asleep each night amid piles of photocopied papers and enormous medical dictionaries, we knew we had to take the bull by the horns. I remember an evening when we looked at each other, and thought, no, no, no – we don't want to do this – we do not want to create a system for this disease. Wasn't it enough to live with it, to cope with it, to walk our kids through it? Couldn't someone else make sense of it, fix it, give us a call when the cure was in? I begged the universe to please take care of us. Nope. Reluctantly, we had to admit that this was our burden. There was no one else.

That decision made, we rolled up our sleeves and plunged in. Using skills I had acquired organising the home-schoolers and counselling college students, we created PXE International in early 1995, an international foundation dedicated to the research of PXE. Of course, there were other organisations dedicated to other diseases, so we sought them out and met with them through the umbrella organisation then called the Alliance for Genetic Support Groups. These other groups told us *not* to try to research the disease, or even influence biomedical research – stick with supporting patients and leave the rest to the professionals. We didn't spend more than a minute spurning this advice. We were also told that if we were going to influence research, it should only be by raising money, and we wouldn't make a dent until we raised hundreds of thousands of dollars. We ignored that too, and made our first grant of the entire $10,000 we raised that first year to the Jackson Laboratories in Bar Harbor Maine, to look for PXE eye signs in mice. They did not find PXE, but did find a naturally occurring mouse model for cataracts. The researcher won a Howard Hughes grant and went on to discover wonderful things in that disease.

Perhaps even stranger in those days was our desire to dig in and get our hands dirty in the lab. Initially, we asked the Harvard researcher who had come to take the kids' blood whether we could 'wash the test tubes in his lab'. We began to go into the lab at about 10pm each night and stay for four or five hours, eventually running experiments designed to find the gene. Concurrently, we pondered the problem of competition and wondered how we could persuade the researchers to collaborate. We had no idea that this was such a vexatious problem – one to which I dedicate a significant amount of my time today.

When I described our vision for collaboration, we were repeatedly told: 'You can't herd cats.' That did it! Yes you can, if you move the food! Clearly, blood, tissue and clinical information from individuals affected by PXE was coveted in this age of gene discovery. All we had to do was to amass this resource in an orderly way, and then the cats would come to us. We could set the rules – to eat you must 'play well with others'. And so, the PXE International Registry and BioBank was born. This was, as far as we know, the first lay-owned blood bank. By the middle of 1995, we were collecting blood and tissue from affected individuals whom we were finding all over the world – through medical conferences, newspaper ads, and outreach to specialists.

The combination of increasing resources in the form of DNA and our hard work through many nights (and we can't forget to thank our neighbour Martha for watching our kids all those nights) resulted in our discovering the gene. I co-authored the gene discovery paper with not one, but two labs, in a back-to-back publication in *Nature Genetics*.

Disappointingly, I couldn't persuade them to collaborate in the end, so this was a creative solution that at least resulted in a tie. I then participated in patenting the gene, as a co-discoverer, and all of the patent holders turned all rights over to PXE International. At that time, I was the only lay person to patent a gene – that may still be the case. I consider myself a steward of the gene, shepherding it through to creating diagnostic tests and trial therapies.

## Towards a Bigger System

We worked over the years, from 1995 to 2004, creating novel solutions, linking up previously adjacent parts of the system. Pat applied his creative systems thinking and construction engineering to the problems and devised a plan that we follow to this day (see the figure below). We engaged in 'disruptive innovation' at every turn, even before it was a popular term. Applying the skills of both advocates and scientists added new levels of engagement to the research enterprise. PXE International adopted aspects of academic models (rigorous science), commercial enterprises (commodification and accountability), and advocacy organisations (trust and agility), and has used them to create a new model for advancing research. I created communities of trust, in both the patient and research communities, and they have been essential and novel.

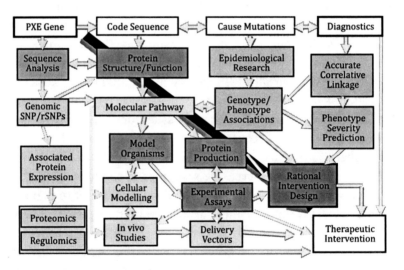

*PXE international strategy.*

As dozens of people came to sit in our living room and ask us to help them found more organisations like PXE International and to create biobanks, we decided (reluctantly, of course) that we should work for bigger systems than this one disease. At first, this was simply by creating common platforms for DNA storage (the Genetic Alliance Registry and BioBank

(biobank.org)), or writing a manual on advocacy that later became Wiki-Advocacy (wikiadvocacy.org). But a critical moment arrived in 2002 that gave new meaning to the phrase 'reluctant entrepreneur' for me.

By this time, I was president of the board of Genetic Alliance (renamed from the early, more narrowly focused 'Alliance for Genetic Support Groups'). Genetic Alliance had broadened its mission and begun to understand that the non-profit world and the world of biomedical research were changing. After all, the human genome sequence had been mapped, and nothing seemed improbable. Cures were around the corner for all of us, were they not?

In 2004, Genetic Alliance experienced a vacancy for the CEO position. I was fired up to find a 'world class leader' to take the organisation to the next level, to blow the lid off, to create the most entrepreneurial non-profit in health one could *not* imagine. I led the board through writing a job description for this creative and tenacious leader. I cranked up the expectations to the point where they matched my vision. I was so excited at the prospect of meeting this person, whom we would find after doing a nationwide search.

The board told me to go home and look in the mirror. NO! We had to look far and wide, there was no mirror involved in this quest. As we searched, they repeatedly told me to look in the mirror. I constantly responded that we needed world-class leadership, not me. After a few months, I realised what my reluctance was about. It was primarily about fear. It was about depending on me to lead, to manifest my vision, but to do that in a transformative way that realised all of the things I was attempting to create outside me – and to do that internally. I feared that looking in that mirror would be a symptom of pride. It was instead, perhaps, the most humble moment of my life to look there and say yes, it is me. I am the world-class leader we have been seeking.

So what of my reluctance to answer the call to become even more entrepreneurial? I found it was based in two things, one easier to deal with than the other. The first has to do with PXE International and the effect of pseudoxanthoma elasticum on my children. It is possible that my decision to work for the larger system will adversely affect them and those living with PXE. It is possible that I will not make the progress I could have on this disease if I decide to work for all diseases.

Two things make this easier to accept. One is that I am convinced that if we work for the larger good, for all disease, for systems in biology, rather than silos, we will advance all causes at an accelerated rate. As President John Kennedy said: 'A rising tide lifts all boats.'

The other is my children's response. At ages 14 and 12, they had admonished us that we would never have meaningful progress until we learned to 'live with disease rather than fight disease', as they did. Thus, they thought that taking charge of Genetic Alliance's destiny would be a healing step for me on that path of learning.

This leads us to the second reason for my reluctance. It is always easy to call excitedly for transformation, reformation, revolution. It is quite another thing to put one's money where one's mouth is – to step up and do it. Taking the CEO position meant I would have to realise my very self. I would have to step into my weakness and lead from it. I would have to inspire by being, rather than proclaiming. Very reluctantly, I became the CEO of Genetic Alliance.

At Genetic Alliance I have led, conspired in, and inspired the transformation of systems. I led the coalition that promoted the Genetic Information Nondiscrimination Act (GINA) of 2008 – a law that Senator Edward Kennedy proclaimed from the floor of the senate as the 'first civil rights law of the new century'. I grew PXE International Registry and BioBank into the aforementioned Genetic Alliance Registry and BioBank. Genetic Alliance established the nation's newborn screening clearing house (babysfirsttest.org). We grew from four staff when I joined Genetic Alliance to more than twenty-two, and were named Washington DC's Best Place to Work in 2010. I can wax lyrical about our accomplishments, but as amazing as they are, they are not the measure of my effectiveness as a reluctant entrepreneur.

During these years, I mistakenly thought that the hero model, and later the rejection of the hero model, was the key to what it meant to be effective. In my hero model years, I purported to be able to take care of everything. I could shoulder the burden of the 7,000+ genetic conditions, and the millions of people affected by them. I could also be the one to empty the trash and buy new pens (not to mention configure the servers, install new computers, book everyone's travel, stay later than everyone else, and come in earlier). I would achieve the goals we

*Senator Ted Kennedy, other lawmakers and NIH Director Francis Collins celebrating the passage of GINA. Photo courtesy of Diane Baker.*

set for unprecedented transformation of the biomedical research and services sectors by brute force and elbow grease! I gradually, and then with greater acceleration, began to see the arrogance in such a hero model – not the typical 'I am great, look at me' ego, but large ego nonetheless. Ego that thought I had to do it all.

This model of leadership was blocking the talents of those around me, removing me from identifying with the system so much that it was outside me. A good example of this is WikiAdvocacy. It is a terrific compendium of information for anyone leading a disease advocacy organisation. Very few people contribute to it, however. When I asked someone who had a hand in developing Wikipedia what they thought the problem was, they said:

> *'It's too well done. When a resource is so well written, so complete, then the community doesn't feel capable of contributing to it. They also don't feel a need to add to it. You will do it. You will take care of them.'*

Wow, what a wake-up call! I believe advocacy overall is burdened by this model and must break it down to be effective in the networked age.

I then vigorously rejected the hero model, and instead created an entirely collaborative model of leadership. In this period, lots of staff and our Council blossomed, but they will tell you that they felt a vacuum of vision and leadership. In this period, staff became hungry for direction. I learned that not everyone has vision, or leadership, and that a balance of these things, in different quantities, made up our vibrant and hard-working staff. The Council and staff learned with me. Some of them have been with Genetic Alliance throughout my entire eight-and-a-half years, with many others for five years or more.

## WHERE FROM HERE?

The practical change that I focus on these days is what we are calling the 'movement'. My work, that of Genetic Alliance, PXE International and the handful of other non-profits I direct, is to contribute to this much larger force emerging in the world of health. The day of organisations leading from the top down is over. It is time for each of us to fully realise our role. In the same way as I wanted to move individuals participating in research from being subjects to being participants, it is now time for each component of the health systems (or lack of systems) to claim a place.

The movement needs leaders who know their place as part of the whole, the *we*. Ordinary people join these leaders in the network age, finding their agency. Vision for working together, creating a movement towards reclaiming health, is emerging in many sectors. Ideas like public access to publicly funded research, rather than locking that information up in journals requiring subscriptions, are ripe and sweeping nations. The UK recently announced that in 2013 all biomedical articles funded by UK grants would be made open access within six months of publication. Major funding agencies have to boldly lead and determine that data sharing should be the norm. Everyone should have the opportunity to share their clinical data from their medical record or clinical trials. Systems are being created to enable cultural transformation of the biomedical enterprise. It is our hope that we can create paths into the new land of collaboration and accelerate the discoveries we need to alleviate suffering in our loved ones.

My family is thriving and entrepreneurialism is woven into its fabric. My husband Pat has founded numerous companies and non-profits. Our daughter Elizabeth has just finished taking PXE International to new levels as the Executive Director and is moving on to new challenges. Our son Ian is balancing high tech (web development) with organic sustainability in a farm he co-owns with us to bring us all healthy food. As he is fond of quoting from the sage Vietnamese Zen master, Thich Nhat Hanh: 'Without mud, there is no lotus'.

My greatest challenge these days is the same as it has always been, but always new. It is myself. I must release myself to be *big*, to be sure, to be humble, to be *one* with others, to be free, to belong, to give freely and to not hold back. I am thrilled to be on this journey and grateful beyond words for my companions on the path. Life is far too short to do anything but go for it.

And though I was reluctant to begin with, and certainly at various points along the way, I know that all of this is a great gift in my life and for the world.

## ACKNOWLEDGEMENTS

I would not be an entrepreneur, reluctant or not, without the incredible people in my life – all of them. I am especially grateful for my partner in life over these twenty-seven years – my husband, Patrick Terry. Our offspring, Elizabeth and Ian, are our teachers, going well beyond my creativity and into a profound and inspired harmony with the earth and its inhabitants.

Kathleen Deignan, CND, my high school teacher and mentor, introduced me to abundant life and Pat: she midwifed the deeper me into being. Kassie and Tom Ruth generously welcomed me into their family life, and the 25 mile bike commute to college was a small price for such a joyful and loving experience. Diane Baker and Francis Collins, fellow journeyers on the path, provide support and respite from all of the challenges in this life. Kemp Battle, my true brother, always propels me forward and is lovingly supportive beyond all expectations. Gene Early, one of the most dedicated truth-seekers I know, boldly brought the new Genetic Alliance into being, creating its culture by boosting us forward

# 10

# BUILDING FOR A BETTER FUTURE

## Wes Janz

*Encounters and conversations with leftover people occupying leftover spaces and using leftover materials, at home and abroad, led architecture professor Wes Janz to view them as urban pioneers, not victims, and teach him a valuable lesson: think small and listen to those at the sharp end.*

Cages. Cage homes actually. 1m × 1m × 2m open-air containers, three high, four floors above Kwun Tong District, Hong Kong 2006. A man cross-legged in the lowest wire-meshed wireframe, head down as we walked through his cage tower neighbourhood. Estimates of 100,000 people living in cages today.

Buenos Aires 2004. If you attended a production at the Cervantes National Theatre you might remember – a woman lived in a sidewalk lean-to built into an oversized pedimented doorway. Tourists and the well-to-do of Argentina looked away as she ate, washed her clothes, and slept in the open. Street theatre redefined.

*Theatre Woman, Buenos Aires, 2006. Photo by author.*

Express train from Delhi, 16.5 hours, slow motion into Mumbai. Daybreak 2001. Thousands of poor. For me, the poorest. People live outside. Wash in dirty puddles. Eat at garbage piles alongside cows and pigs. Dozens of men squat at the rail line. They defecate, urinate and yawn as we clickety-clack, clickety-clack to the station.

Many cities are undergoing extraordinary growth with millions of residents living in conditions unknown to others more privileged. People are hungry, thirsty. They need places to work, sleep, love, play. They deserve health care, public transportation, safe drinking water and sanitation, schools, land rights. Some are on the move to keep ahead of war, ethnic cleansing, religious persecution or famine. Others want just a chance, just an opportunity for their children. Many of the newest arrivals are looking for families or family friends, maybe living on the pavement for the first days or weeks until they find a place, maybe an informal settlement.

According to UN-Habitat, the numbers are big. More than one billion people live in slums worldwide (with another one billion expected by

2030). 'Mega-regions' or 'endless cities' are forming with populations in excess of one hundred million. Every day 180,000 people urbanise.

Every day.

And every day, including this day, is a struggle for most men, women and children.

In a way that is both unsettling and engaging, you come to understand: nearly every person will achieve the most basic of successes. He or she will find something to eat. Jobs will be worked. Houses will be built. Whether from a cage, a lean-to, or alongside railroad tracks as a new day dawns, people get on with their lives.

We have no choice. This is what we do.

There's a complementary shrinking process grinding on older cities in Europe, the countries of the former Soviet Union and the post-industrial Rust Belt. According to the *Atlas of Shrinking Cities,* since 1950 more than 350 large cities have lost a significant number of inhabitants. Greater London and Tokyo have lost over a million residents, and 400,000 have gone from Detroit, Chicago, New York, Philadelphia and St. Louis in the last fifty years.

It's not a pretty sight. But this break up needs to be seen. With colleague Olon Dotson, I organised two week-long student caravans: the 'Midwess Distress Tour' (2006) to Detroit, Flint, Gary, Chicago, East St. Louis and Cincinnati; and the 'Distress Too Tour' (2008) to Youngstown, Wilkes-Barre, Scranton, Philadelphia, Braddock and Camden.

These are cities with worn out infrastructures, architectures and residents. The people who remain do so in places no longer on anyone's 'bucket list' unless your curiosities include (in alphabetical order): abandonment, abuse, arson, bankruptcy, chronic unemployment, corner stores, corruption, declining tax base, demolition, drop-out rates, early death, felonies, foreclosures, homicide, 'most dangerous US cities', Packard, prostitution, receivership, ruin porn, scandal, sideways drift. And worse.

In time – after numerous sidewalk chats and chance encounters – I came to see any person who stays – anyone – not as a victim, not as a creature deserving sympathy, not as someone to be feared, but as an urban pioneer committed to a city many deserted.

Detroit 2011. Urban prairie, 2600 block, Pierce Street. Four houses remain, two vacated in the last two years. Bessie, 96, in bathrobe. Her 'What cha'll doin' here?' to students and me starts a fifteen-minute chat. We stand in the street, there's no traffic. She's in this house for over fifty years. 'Finish school!' is her parting shot to the students. (Next time in Detroit, I'll check to see whether she's still there.)

East St. Louis 2012. Myra has volunteered to lead the clean up of the long-gone Booker T. Washington black cemetery in nearby Centreville. She takes us there. Untended for decades, it's a dumping ground for all sorts of crap tossed indiscriminately in a place defined by discrimination. Among those interred are 500 black babies buried in the 1940s, victims of a plague, graves now covered with flood plain overwash.

*Outdoor oven, Braddock, Pennsylvania, 2008. Photo by author.*

Braddock 2008. This borough in the Pittsburgh metro area, in 1920, was home to 20,000. It now holds just over 2,000. But those who remain now have an outdoor bread-baking oven; conceived by Ray and built of recycled brick, block and stones from nearby demolitions and arsons.

Materials destined for the landfill now produce herb-spiced breads and pizzas, host open-air book readings and wine tastings.

Cities exploding and cities shrinking. The scale of the challenges we face – the relentless march of urbanisation, the steady drip, drip, drip of jobs and people out of distress – suggest that we must move away from the ways of thinking that brought us to this moment. We've listened to the same voices, privileged the same precedents and accepted the same logic systems long enough.

Putting patches on what's already broken – that's the paradigm lived by Bessie, Myra and Ray.

We must look at new works, unconventional processes, and ask questions from other perspectives.

It is time for an informed iconoclasm.

It is time to look elsewhere.

Thinking through pain and possibilities I couldn't have imagined, I struggled to make sense of what I'd seen, of what I'd come to believe. I came to the word and category: leftover.

This is how a dictionary defines 'leftover': something that remains as residue or unconsumed. A thesaurus lists synonyms: remainder (rubbish, odd, waste); and excess (surplus, bonus, dividend). The leftover is a fertile category that takes in shared understandings of waste and rubbish as it recasts excess people, odd spaces and found debris as outstanding, bonuses or dividends. Your garbage is my prize, a wasted space welcomes our event and someone asking for spare change has potential. Believing in a leftover person occupying leftover spaces and building with leftover materials inverts conventional sensibilities. We stop giving people what we think they need. The discourse becomes more honest: intelligence resides with us and with them. People are engaged, not as consumers, but as co-constructors of knowledge.

What we know. Informal settlers worldwide: one billion and rising. Tokyo and London: down by one million. Urbanise daily: 180,000 plus.

This writing is not about them, not exactly.

It is not about billions, millions, thousands, hundreds, or even tens.

It is about one.

September 2006. There's an open jar of peanut butter on the porch's top step, a white plastic knife the marker of a man disappeared mid-meal. Maybe he's always mid-meal. Or between meals. 417 Second Avenue, Flint, Michigan. Shopping carts, blue and red, nestle against the bottom step. Plastic milk crates, one upside down to support the peanut butter place setting. Blankets hang in the porch's openings.

Squatter defined: somebody who occupies land or property illegally, especially somebody who takes over and lives in somebody else's empty house.

Glenn says, 'Don't touch anything.'

The squatter, though an illegal occupant, has rights. These are his things. This is his peanut butter, his white plastic knife. We can't pack them up, jack him out. This porch is his, for now. We're walking into his home, without his permission, checking out where he sleeps, what he eats, his furniture, his 'I Am Me ... I Am Okay' poster. What you keep to yourself, he doesn't get to. Can't.

*Keith Austin porch dwelling, Flint, Michigan, 2006. Photo by author.*

The neighbours are complaining, not to the police (there are no longer enough of them and they've got more serious criminals to chase), but to the Genesee County Land Bank (the owners of the foreclosed property), and Glenn is sent to evict Keith from his squat. I happen to be there with graduate students.

Unexpectedly, Keith appeared. We talked as he loaded a shopping cart with his belongings, on his way to a new squat. (This was the first time for all the students – originating from Egypt, India, Indonesia and Nepal – to talk with a squatter.) People in the neighbourhood, according to Keith, give him jobs. That's how he survives. When he is too cold, they give him shelter and blankets.

*Keith Austin (centre), Flint, Michigan, 2006. Photo by author.*

True story. When our group was on the porch, a man veered his automobile to the kerb and demanded to know 'Is Keith dead?'

At one point, Keith said to us, 'I know where to get food and water. I know how to hunt.' A student whispered to me, 'Perhaps being an urban squatter is like living in the wild.'

Squatter defined: a person or animal that crouches down.

When we departed, Keith – a squatter, no less – said to me, 'You can get as much as you want out of life. I believe in being positive.'

People get on with their lives. They have no choice.

Keith knows what is best.

Should we listen to Keith?

# THE IMPORTANCE OF MY EARLY LIFE

I'm a licensed architect, a professor of architecture, and I earned a PhD. But my early days were something else and have resonated with me ever more.

I'm a rural kid, raised on a thirty-two-hectare farm in central Wisconsin (500 kilometres north-northwest of Chicago), the youngest of three children. Dad and mom were poor and left school after ninth grade to support their families. My dad, Hersel, was an everyday innovator. There was no reluctance, no choice. A broken machine? He fixed it. A sick animal? He nursed it. An empty cheque book? He worked at a

*The author and his father Hersel on the family farm, 1958. Photo courtesy of author.*

paper-making factory. 'Fun' was simple: card games, a cheap beer, jokes at the paper mill. My mother, Bert, scrambled, salvaged, made do. Socks were darned, clothes were patched, and her 'better' outfits were self-tailored even as she worked alongside dad in the fields and barns. Most of our food was grown on-site: vegetables, fruits, chickens and cattle. House, barn and machine shed were supplemented with add-ons, lean-tos, in-betweens ... a corn crib, a two-stall horse barn, a chicken coop, a milk house remodel, a new garage. We were self-builders, bartering services and skills with cousin Elmer, uncle Felix and friend Oscar.

Memories. Mom's treat to me: bacon grease spread on store-bought white bread, sprinkled with sugar. First grade: walking one kilometre to a rural one-room schoolhouse, eight grades, two outhouses, one hand water pump. Hersel's broken body language when his cattle (to whom he gave names) were shipped to slaughter. Surgery on a standing cow, its hide peeled back in layers to remove from its stomachs the nails, staples and pieces of wire eaten along the pasture's fence line. Isolated for days in pure white, waiting for the snow plough's rescue.

Dad died in 1993 and Mom in 2002, both from cancer. I was close to my parents. Their deaths worked on me, stripped me of any notion that I could or should control everything.

My doctoral dissertation, completed in 1995, is titled 'Building Nations by Designing Buildings'. It captures the intentions and actions of an impressive power elite as they controlled the creation of 'the cultural centre of the world', Lincoln Center for the Performing Arts in New York City. I focused on the architectural office of Eero Saarinen and Associates. Why were they selected to design the Vivian Beaumont Repertory Theater? How did the client direct the architects? Why did the theatre – as a critically disappointing project in this prominent architect's portfolio – become one of Saarinen's leftovers? That is, it too is often ignored and I thought it might provide alternative understandings of this architect's processes and products.

Then, I was curious about the power held by the world's wealthiest individuals and most prominent designers.

Three pushes took me to different concerns. One, my parents' deaths. Two, the beginnings of a decade of travelling to south Asia and Latin America. Three, a ten-year stint as director of a post-professional Master of Architecture programme that enrolled students from Argentina, China, Colombia, Egypt, Germany, India, Indonesia, Mexico, Nepal, Panama, Serbia, Sri Lanka, Thailand, Turkey and the USA. I came to believe that most people are perfectly capable of making their way and that it is often the case that the interventions of well-intentioned people bring both opportunity and harm to the lives of locals who are seen as being 'poor' or 'disadvantaged'. I began to work bottom-up, one person and one small project at a time.

Now, I take seriously the displaced family, the claimed space and the salvaged brick. It's the cascading energies of small responses and helping moments, repeated, that interest me.

## THE IMPACT OF MY IDEAS

I'm an educator and an architect. To focus on 'impact', I'll overview three activities: thesis projects on which I was the major adviser; the construction of 'small architectures' (as framed by a leftover materials approach); and a small architecture inspired by the material sensibility practiced every day by self-builders around the world – a garage that is possibly the first permanent building in the USA made almost exclusively of timber pallets with the authorisation of a formal building permit.

*About graduate thesis projects.* On several recent trips to Detroit (with students) I met with Grace Lee Boggs, a 98-year-old lifelong activist. Her autobiography, *Living for Change*, includes this distinction:

> *'Rebellion is a stage in the development of revolution but it is not revolution... A rebellion disrupts the society but it does not provide what is necessary to make a revolution and establish a new social order. To make a revolution, people ... must make a philosophical/spiritual leap and become more human human beings. In order to change/transform the world, they must change/transform themselves.'*

Such an approach – to not demand change from others, but instead to participate in my own transformation into a more human human being – well, this deep questioning challenged my teaching and is a challenge I bring to my students. Dozens of thesis explorations, for which I served as major adviser, came to be grounded in the interrelated issues of personal humanity, empathy, repurposing found material systems, contested space, expanding building typologies and future work. Among those completed are these ten (in chronological order).

According to Kathrin Löer, those typically considered to be homeless in Berlin 'are not homeless. For the 'city users', the city becomes home – the home city.' Her 2006 thesis, 'At Home With the Unhoused: Conversations With Men and Women Living on the Streets of Berlin', concludes: 'We – architects, designers, planners, policy makers, and others – have much to learn from those we consider to be homeless.'

Tülay Günes (2006), in her thesis 'Portable Houses and Context: The Case of Israeli Settlements in the West Bank', studied the 'political and social practice of placing [portable houses] in one of the world's most contested territories – the West Bank.'

In 2007, Chandra Shrestha's thesis, 'Advanced Technology in a Low Technology Setting', speculated on the potential of implementing advanced Building Information Modelling (BIM) software into several low technology settings found in the rural building construction processes in his home country of Nepal.

Inspired by meeting Keith in Flint, in 2007 Marwa el-Ashmouni's key thesis question became: Will architecture be able to activate this self-builder spirit by reusing some of the materials left over from the house demolition process?

'A conversation with Antoine, a local resident, became the turnkey moment. I found an intellectual connection based in the casual interaction of like-minded, passionate citizens.' So wrote Derek Mills in his 2009 thesis, 'Material Re-Sourcing: A Systematic Approach to Re-Creation Within Urban Decay'.

> 'As the conversation was directed towards the feelings and objectives through the eyes of Antoine, and where he perceived his community moving, I was able to discuss my design knowledge as a 'person' and not as an 'architect'. This realisation grounded a new way of thinking about how I should present, illustrate, construct and engage my design knowledge without all the conventional architectural undertones. My basic conclusion from talking with Antoine: architects should reconsider who we position as the most important client.'

Gabriela Valencia, with 'From Rural to Urban: Studying Informal Settlements in Panama' (2009), asked 'what physical and spatial sensibilities rural people might bring with them when migrating to large cities. The specific case is Ms Emilia [the domestic worker who helped to raise Gabriela] and her move from Sona to Panama City. In addition, a typology of five settlement patterns in Panama City are described and a small design intervention is proposed for each.'

Tayler Mikosz and Ashley VanMeter, with their 2011 thesis, 'Potentialising: A Challenge in Thinking and Making', argued that it 'is time to define used materials in a way that provides a clear connection to the ever-changing profession of architecture and its responsibility to the earth and to humanity.'

Jason Klinker's 2011 thesis is titled 'Engaging Them. Becoming Us. An Architect's Role'. To better become 'us', he worked one day a week at a local soup kitchen where he came to know those who frequented the kitchen and engaged the locals in a re-modelling of their facilities.

'From the Ground Up: Reimagining the Packard Auto Plant in Detroit, Michigan', as proposed by Matt Amore in 2011, 'nurtur[ed] the small-scale entrepreneurship already happening in the neighborhood and promot[ed] a new educational model focused on the inherent creativity and sense of purpose to be found in local people.'

'I am the ice cream lady', said Veronica Eulacio to begin her 2012 thesis presentation. Inspired by a woman living in an informal settlement near Caracas, in her home country of Venezuela, Veronica's proposal, The Potential of the Forgotten, reveals human possibilities on urban, neighbourhood, sidewalk and vending cart scales.

I have been a university professor for eighteen years. It's obvious that many of the architecture students in this generation see a more humanistic role for themselves. The connections they make with people living in expanding or shrinking cities will not be easily forgotten. Kathrin, Tülay, Chandra, Marwa, Derek, Gabriela, Tayler, Ashley, Jason, Matt, and Veronica … each is a more human human being now. And that is a good place from which to begin a revolutionary's work.

*About small architectures.* Squatters 'mix more concrete than any developer. They lay more bricks than any government… Squatters are the largest builders of housing in the world – and they are creating the cities of tomorrow.'

With that one paragraph from his 2005 book, *Shadow Cities*, Robert Neuwirth galvanised my retooling. To research his book, Neuwirth lived in informal settlements in Istanbul, Mumbai, Nairobi and Rio de Janeiro, each for six months. As I learned about the complexity present in the lives of 'shadow city' residents in the settlements where he lived and the settlements I visited, I thought: why not be a part of the world's largest construction force?

At that moment, there was no hesitation. No reluctance.

I came back to a basic bit of personal identity: I'm an architect. And so I began designing and building within the constraints and potentials of what I found in the underutilised spaces of cities and our gargantuan solid waste stream. The fact is, I'd already begun some small constructional efforts to sort out new understandings and questions.

2001. An award-winning arbour made almost exclusively of found materials (branches and items set out by neighbours, objects donated by friends, artefacts from my parents' vacated house), with collaborators Jerome Daksiewicz and Sohith Perera.

*Arbour, Indianapolis, Indiana, 2004. Photo by author.*

2002. Bus shelters for Bloomington, Indiana. In a geologic area that is a world centre of limestone quarrying, Jerome and I visited quarries, spoke with limestone workers, studied the logic of gang saws and proposed a design incorporating flawed (and worthless) 'roughback' blocks.

2002. Sixteen dwellings, made only of scavenged materials, each constructed on campus by a graduate student in our 'Leftover Spaces, Leftover Materials, Leftover People' design studio. All the students occupied their shelters for five days and nights. (I too lived and slept outside for the project's duration, in 4°C weather.)

2003. Two pavilions at the University of Moratuwa in Colombo, Sri Lanka, one of scavenged wood (packing crates, pallets and tree trunks), the other of earthen materials (including masonry rubble from demolished campus buildings), designed and built as part of the CapAsia field study programme created and directed by Dr Nihal Perera at Ball State University.

2003. 'Bocetos espacios modularies' (or space sketches) – three installations in Buenos Aires and Rosario, Argentina constructed spontaneously, and exclusively of string, with colleagues Jerome Daksiewicz, Ana de Brea, Adam Janusz and Devin McConkey.

2004. Six structures built by architecture students and professors in a four-day workshop, using only timber pallets and hand tools. Primary organisers included Azin Valy and Suzan Wines, partners in I-Beam Design, whose 'Pallet House' competition entry featured reused pallets to provide transitional housing in war-torn Kosovo.

*Timber pallet workshop, Ball State University,*
*Muncie, Indiana, 2004. Photo by author.*

2005. 'Catalysing' construction of thirty permanent houses, post-tsunami, in Kalametiya, Sri Lanka, using hand tools to dig trenches for granite foundations. Participants: hundreds of local villagers, twenty-one US-based CapAsia students, and colleagues Nihal Perera and Timothy Gray.

*Rebuilding Kalametiya, Sri Lanka, 2005. Photos by author.*

2006. At the invitation of my mentor Robert Beckley and the Genesee Research Institute in Flint, Michigan, I moved from construction to the deconstruction of abandoned houses, shifting my attention to the re-making of distressed Rust Belt neighbourhoods, cities and lives.

2010. I curated the 'small architecture BIG LANDSCAPES' show at the Swope Art Museum in Terre Haute, Indiana. Fifty international, national and local colleagues contributed built installations, drawings, paintings, photographs or essays. Participants were asked 'to consider some of our most extreme and, simultaneously, most common architecture and landscapes' as part of a larger argument that 'we have much to learn from those generally considered to be the most disadvantaged.' Among the highlights: six 'small architectures' and collections of self-builder tools and profiles from Canada, Honduras, Nepal, Panama, Thailand and Turkey. This show later travelled to Ball State University, Central Michigan University, University of Minnesota and University of Wisconsin-Milwaukee.

2012. I curated 'Couched Constructions' at the Herron School of Art and Design in Indianapolis. This 'found couch show' offered three levels of exploration. In a three-hour workshop, teams played with material systems commonly found kerbside: hard-shell suitcases, chairs and stools, small tables, containers with handles, or umbrellas. The second level: couch installations completed by teams from Ball State University, Indiana University, Tuskegee University and the University of Kentucky, along with several local architects. Each installation represented a significant commitment of time and design thinking to the gallery-quality outcomes. Level three was a full-scale prototype of Pallet

Garage. It represented ten years of thinking and building regarding one found material system. In this sense, the show included the beginning, middle and (conditional) end of a coordinated set of found material explorations conducted over a ten-year period.

This portfolio of small architectures is, for me, a series of small trials, a working through of energies related to constraints as they came up against conventional architectural sensibilities regarding aesthetics, economics, craft, technology, scheduling and audience. I was building small architecture and confidence. I now know that what I know and question as an architect is of value within a world of extreme limits. And I know that who I am as a more human human being can matter not only to what I do with my life, time and work, but to other people as well.

*About Pallet Garage.* A garage we completed in Indianapolis in 2012 is very probably the first permanent building in the USA to be constructed almost entirely of timber pallets and granted a building permit (STR11-02978, City of Indianapolis, Department of Code Enforcement, August 26, 2011).

Pallets are omnipresent. My students and I found pallets in the small architectures of informal settlers in Buenos Aires, Chihuahua, Istanbul and Panama City, and in the blogs of self-builders throughout North America and Europe. Urban pioneers in falling Rust Belt cities reclaim pallets and shape composting frames, gardening hot boxes and chicken coops. Farmers use pallets to build sheds, fences and more. And architects – including Avatar Architettura, I-Beam Design, Köbberling and Kaltwasser, ManosArchitects, Onix and Project Iceberg – contribute temporary pavilions and museum installations.

To the best of my knowledge, however, these builders have not negotiated the gap between informal and formal economies with a permanent pallet building authorised by a building permit.

Stepping back. Pallet Garage is part of the larger 'Cabin(s) in the Woods' project, involving renovation of a small limestone house and construction of a second small timber frame house. These 'cabins' are connected by a seven-metre glass corridor, all on a small plateau of a heavily wooded and ravined one-hectare site seventy blocks north of downtown Indianapolis. The garage anchors the project's southern edge, shapes the pedestrian sequence from off-site into the house and illuminates the entry courtyard. Among the constraints accepted: to use only industry standard 40' x 48' wood pallets; to follow a kit of parts approach with fully, partially and unassembled pallets; to know pallet production processes and producers; and to anticipate that the details and constructions on the Pallet Garage must be possible on sites in neighbourhoods worldwide where only hand tools are available and heavy lifting is done not by industrialised machine, but by strong backs. We did not demand nor design a 'new' pallet to meet our needs; rather, we utilised the potential of the most conventional pallet to fulfil criteria for both quality (and ease) of construction and quality of spatial experience by those of severely limited means.

My colleagues: Paul Puzzello, Tayler Mikosz, Ashley VanMeter, Steve Kessinger, Scott Szentes, Andrea Swartz, Jon Schwab and Randy King.

*Pallet Garage, Indianapolis, Indiana, 2011/12. Photos by author.*

Working drawings of Pallet Garage (including a Structural Sheet for the three-dimensional rafters, as submitted by consulting engineers) were posted online on August 1, 2011 for free use worldwide.

Going forward. It is my hope that by open sourcing the design we will enable self-builders worldwide, even those without Internet access, but who are in contact with local NGOs and non-profits, to benefit from this small demonstration project.

Pallet Garage is an argument on behalf of the inspiration of the designers and builders of the slum, the deserted neighbourhood and the farmer, and also bears witness to the knowledge architects and engineers can bring to such found material systems, as it shares such minimal, but meaningful, improvement with current building and urban practitioners in Indianapolis, the USA and the rest of the world.

## WHAT'S NEXT FOR THIS IDEA AND ME?

Yes, construction of Pallet Garage is Step 2 of what I hope is a six-step journey.

*Step 1. Design the pallet building and post drawings online.*

*Step 2. Construct the garage.*

*Step 3. Disseminate 'How to build with timber pallets' online to targeted NGOs, non-profits and others concerned with construction worldwide.*

*Step 4. Accept invitation to build a small timber pallet project somewhere in the world. (I'm waiting for that invitation.)*

*Step 5. Build one small pallet project alongside locals, leveraging my architectural intelligence within local building practices.*

*Step 6. Repeat Steps 4 and 5.*

Yes, I intend to be a 'radical humanist'. In early July 2012 I finished reading Manning Marable's new book, *Malcolm X: A Life of Reinvention*. Marable observes that part of Malcolm X's legacy might be 'the politics of radical humanism.' A 'deep respect for, and a belief in, black humanity was at the heart of this revolutionary visionary's faith' that in time 'expanded to include people of divergent nationalities and racial identities... Malcolm X should become a representative for hope and human dignity.' These days, my reluctance is flipping to readiness, anticipation, openness ... I'm reluctant to keep doing what I've already done and wondering what else can be. I'm now asking: what might be the evidence that one is 'radical' as a humanist-educator and as a humanist-architect?

And yes, I'll return to many of the places I've cited in this writing and hope I'll have a chance to reconnect with some of the people I've mentioned and meet some new ones. I'm most interested in longitudinal relationships with people and places, in coming to know and be known over time. I start there, and if it matters, in time, that I'm an architect, so be it.

## CHALLENGES I FACE

The architecture profession, because it is an economic creation, values profit. Humans are de-humanised as concerns about per-square-metre costs, billable hours, occupant loads and facility 'users' dominate. Most architects are drawn to the material aspects of building; concerns for the social, cultural, or political realms – for people – are often secondary, if considered at all.

Each architect and architecture student is the product of an enculturating and professionalising (and highly Westernised) set of conventions that dominate curriculum, accreditation and licensure issues worldwide. What it means to be different or offer another perspective is considered, of course, but within norms widely accepted and little discussed.

Architecture schools understandably focus on the young learner, not the local person. Well-intentioned students and professors often design 'for' someone else viewed as aspiring to, or in need of, the middle class lifestyle and values of the student, professor or architect. Sympathy rules and projects are often based in preconceptions, generalities and a belief that the educated Westerner knows best.

I wonder, do architecture professors and students need poor people more than poor people need architecture professors and students?

Are architects the people in need, the disadvantaged, the ones at risk? The ones who are 'poor'?

I am reminded of something said to me in 2006, standing among a number of 'house piles' (houses so long abandoned that nature is pulling them back to the earth) and chatting kerbside with Dorothy in East St. Louis: 'Professor, we don't need to be studied. We need help.'

Robert Neuwirth, in his 2011 book, *Stealth of Nations: The Global Rise of the Informal Economy*, writes of 'System D' – 'the inventive, self-starting, entrepreneurial merchants who are doing business on their own, without registering or being regulated by bureaucracy.'

Three years after my first trip to East St. Louis, we found a 'D' crew of self-starters a ten-minute drive from where Dorothy and I spoke.

Theirs is a place that is a 'no place', really. The last thing these guys want is anyone asking questions, or getting noticed by the bureaucracy, or any sort of social media presence. Ten or so push lawn mowers lined up for repair. Fifty timber pallets stacked for resale. A forklift to move pallets. A small steel salvage yard. Smoke in the air, so something cooking, probably ribs. Men playing cards, gambling. We didn't get past 'What's goin' on?' No one talking to Olon or me ... either 'the boss is gone' or somebody grunted at us. Stonewalled, we left. But three years later, in 2012, we returned and saw the same place, same set-up, probably the same crew, the same card game.

Every day I think about how to help (and not study) Dorothy. If I had the chance, there are ten related questions I'd ask these men:

1. Why are you guys still in East St. Louis?
2. Why does the City leave you alone (if they do)?
3. Who owns this land?
4. How much money are you making?
5. Who are your clients?
6. I don't see chain link fences. How do you secure your stuff?
7. Any advantages to joining the formal economy?
8. If you imagine expanding your entrepreneurship, what's next?
9. How can you become more productive, efficient and effective?
10. Are the ribs ready?

Here, I very much like a statement by M. Scott Ball, an architecture professor at Tulane University, in his piece, Expanding the Role of the Architect: 'If it looks like it could use the help of an architect, it probably is architecture.'

Maybe the 'D' Crew could use the help of an architect. Maybe it is architecture. So, next time in East St. Louis, I'll say to these cats:

- I'm an architect. Does that mean anything to your businesses?
- I'm an architect. Ever think of building with those pallets?

- I'm an architect. I can hook you up with entrepreneurs in Mumbai.
- I'm an architect. Anybody have construction experience?
- I'm an architect. Can I order found materials through you?

I'd 'help' by making the challenges faced every day by local people the challenges I'd face with them as an architect.

## ADVICE FOR ANYONE WANTING TO START OUT IN SOCIAL INNOVATION

Don't do anything.

Hesitate. Doubt. Be unsure. Be undecided.

In other words, be reluctant.

People determined to 'do something', or 'change the world' or 'make a difference' in someone else's life … well, these folks scare me. Too often it is the case that the interventions of well-intentioned people are soon ignored by or bring harm to locals. Sometimes the best thing we can do for someone else (and ourselves) is to walk away. Let it be. Let them be.

Don't be in a hurry to start a non-profit. Don't do an internship at the World Bank, in the Eurozone, or for the United Nations. Don't apply to graduate schools. Don't start yet another blog for social innovators.

Not yet.

Next time you're pan-handled downtown, saddened by the lunch line-up outside the soup kitchen, or come face-to-face with the night shifter who cleans the toilets in your office or building, I advise:

Be a radical humanist.

Be a more human human being.

Extend a hand. Offer your name. Listen to the reply.

Come to know one person, a stranger, on a first name basis.

Let's try together.

'Hi. My name is Wes.'

'What's yours?'

# About the Authors

## Foreword: Archbishop Desmond Tutu

Archbishop Desmond Tutu is a Nobel Peace Laureate and former Archbishop of Cape Town who played a key role in the fight against apartheid in South Africa. In 1995, President Nelson Mandela appointed him Chairman of the Truth and Reconciliation Commission, a body set up to probe gross human rights violations that occurred under apartheid. Today, Archbishop Tutu is considered an elder world statesman and is widely regarded as a moral voice promoting peace, reconciliation and justice.

## Introduction: Ken Banks

Ken Banks, Founder of kiwanja.net, devotes himself to the application of mobile technology for positive social and environmental change, and has spent the last two decades working on projects in Africa. His early research resulted in the development of FrontlineSMS, an award-winning text message communication system today powering thousands of social change projects in over one hundred and fifty countries around the world.

Following a management transition at FrontlineSMS in mid-2012, Ken has been focusing on a new project, Means of Exchange, which looks at how everyday technologies can be used to democratise opportunities for economic self-sufficiency, rebuild local community and promote a return to local resource use.

Ken graduated from Sussex University with honours in Social Anthropology with Development Studies, was awarded a Stanford University Reuters Digital Vision Fellowship in 2006, and named a PopTech Social Innovation Fellow in 2008. In 2009 he was named a Laureate of the Tech Awards, an international awards programme which honours innovators from around the world who are applying technology to benefit humanity. He was named a National Geographic Emerging Explorer in May 2010 and an Ashoka Fellow in 2011, and was the recipient of the 2011 Pizzigati Prize for Software in the Public Interest. That summer he won the Curry Stone Design Prize for his pioneering work with FrontlineSMS, and was selected as a member of the UK Prime Minister's delegation to Africa. In 2012 the Cambridge business community presented Ken with a 'Special Achievement Award' for his work as a social entrepreneur. Later that year he was made a Fellow of the Royal Society of Arts.

Ken represents Sussex University as their Ambassador for International Development, and is a founding member of the British Government Department for International Development's 'Digital Advisory Board'. In addition to his own work, Ken mentors early-stage entrepreneurs through PopTech and the Unreasonable Institute.

Ken is also well known for his writing and blogging on Africa, technology and innovation and his work has been published online by CNN, the BBC and the Guardian among others. He has also written for the print edition of *Wired* magazine, and has had guest chapters published in a number of collaborative books. When he's not working, Ken spends much of his time being bossed around by his young son, Henry, and twins Madeleine and Oliver.

**Website:** kiwanja.net
**Twitter:** @kiwanja | @MeansofExchange

## CHAPTER 1: BRIJ KOTHARI

Brij Kothari is on the faculty of the Indian Institute of Management, Ahmedabad (IIM-A) and the founder of PlanetRead.org (non-profit) and BookBox.com (for-profit), both dedicated to literacy and language learning through popular culture, mass media and Information and Communication Technologies.

At IIM-A and PlanetRead, Brij and his team have innovated, researched and implemented Same Language Subtitling (SLS) on television for mass literacy. SLS on Bollywood film songs delivers reading practice to 200 million early-readers in India, prompting Bill Clinton to call it 'a small change that has a staggering impact on people's lives.' He has represented his SLS work at the Clinton Global Initiative in New York (2009 and 2011) and the World Economic Forum in Davos (2011 and 2013).

BookBox produces animated stories for children, integrated with SLS to deliver reading and language learning in over thirty languages. BookBox content is freely available on YouTube.

Brij was elected Schwab Foundation Indian Social Entrepreneur of the Year (2009), Ashoka Fellow (2004) and Reuters Digital Vision Fellow at Stanford University (2003). His research publications have primarily focused on literacy, primary education and indigenous knowledge. He is a regular columnist on social innovation and entrepreneurship for the *Financial Chronicle*.

The SLS innovation recently won the 2013 International Prize of the Library of Congress Literacy Awards. It is also the recipient of awards from the All Children Reading Grand Challenge (USAID), Tech Museum of Innovation (San Jose), the Institute for Social Inventions (London), Development Marketplace (World Bank) and the NASSOM Foundation (Social Innovation Honour). Brij is a Finalist for the World Technology Award for Education (2013).

Brij grew up in the Sri Aurobindo Ashram in Pondicherry, India. He has a PhD in Education and a Masters in Development Communication from Cornell University, and a Masters in Physics from the Indian Institute of Technology, Kanpur.

**Website:** PlanetRead.org
**Twitter:** @Brij_PlanetRead

## CHAPTER 2: ERIK HERSMAN

Erik Hersman is an entrepreneur, writer and speaker on the boundless spirit of technology innovation in Africa. He is the co-founder of Ushahidi, which allows users to share breaking news through text messaging that continues to revolutionise and empower journalists, watchdog groups, and everyday people around the world. He also founded the iHub in Nairobi, the innovation hub for the technology community, which is bringing together entrepreneurs, hackers, designers and the investment community and is built around the vision of an epicentre for Kenya's booming tech industry. He is also the founder of the BRCK, a new connectivity device that is considered a back-up generator for the Internet, and is a general partner in the Savannah Fund, which makes small seed investments in Africa's tech start-ups.

A TED Senior Fellow and PopTech Faculty Fellow, Erik grew up in Kenya and Sudan and keeps two influential blogs: WhiteAfrican, where he writes about technology on the African continent, and AfriGadget, a group blog that celebrates African ingenuity.

**Website:** whiteafrican.com
**Twitter:** @whiteafrican | @AfriGadget | @Ushahidi |
        @iHub | @BRCKnet

## CHAPTER 3: JOEL SELANIKIO

Dr Joel Selanikio leads DataDyne's efforts to develop and promote new technologies and business models for health and international development, including multiple award-winning Magpi mobile data collection software (formerly EpiSurveyor) – the most widely scaled mobile technology ever created for international development, with over 24,000 users in more than 170 countries.

Dr Selanikio is a frequent speaker and consultant in the fields of social entrepreneurship, innovation, public health and the use of technology for development ('ICT4D'). He is a judge for the GSMA Global Mobile Awards, was named by Forbes as one of the most powerful innovators of 2009, and is a winner of the Lemelson–MIT Award for Sustainability and the Wall Street Journal Technology Innovation Award.

He has been profiled by *The Guardian, Wired, Forbes, The Economist, The Wall Street Journal,* the BBC and *The Washington Post,* among many others. His public speaking includes presentations at The World Economic Forum in Davos, TED, Foo Camp, Google, Clinton Global Initiative, the Royal Society of Medicine, SciFoo and many other venues.

Dr Selanikio is a practising paediatrician, as well as a former Wall Street computer consultant, and former CDC epidemiologist. In his role as an officer of the Public Health Service, Dr Selanikio served as Chief of Operations for the HHS Secretary's Emergency Command Centre in the aftermath of 9/11. In 2005, he was given the Haverford Award for Humanitarian Service for his work in treating tsunami victims in Aceh, Indonesia.

**Website:**  about.me/jselanikio
**Twitter:**  @jselanikio | @datadyne

## Chapter 4: Josh Nesbit

Josh Nesbit is the CEO and co-founder of Medic Mobile, a non-profit technology company on a mission to improve health equity in underserved communities. Medic Mobile supports 10,000 community health workers across nineteen countries in Africa, Asia, Latin America and the USA. Josh also created Hope Phones, a cell phone recycling campaign designed to engage millions of Americans. He is an Ashoka Fellow, PopTech Social Innovation Fellow, Echoing Green Fellow and Rainer Arnhold Fellow. Josh was selected by Devex as one of 40 Under 40 Leaders in International Development, received the Truman Award for Innovation from the Society for International Development and was named by Forbes in 2011 as one of the world's top thirty social entrepreneurs.

**Website:**  medicmobile.org
**Twitter:**  @joshnesbit | @medic

## CHAPTER 5: LAURA STACHEL

Dr Laura Stachel, co-founder and executive director of We Care Solar, is a board-certified obstetrician-gynaecologist with fourteen years of clinical experience. She holds an MD from the University of California, San Francisco and an MPH in Maternal and Child Health from the University of California, Berkeley. Her research on maternal mortality in Nigeria in 2008 alerted her to the deleterious effects of energy poverty on maternal health outcomes. Along with Hal Aronson, she co-founded We Care Solar to bring simple solar electric solutions to maternal and child health care in regions without reliable electricity. We Care Solar has equipped hundreds of health facilities in more than twenty-five countries with the Solar Suitcase, a compact solar energy system providing essential lighting and power.

Laura is passionate about promoting sustainable energy solutions for women's health and speaks around the world on this topic. She has been active in the UN Foundation's Sustainable Energy for All Initiative and co-chairs the Working Group on Energy and Health. Laura is one of the Top 10 CNN Heroes of 2013. For her work with We Care Solar, Laura received the 2012 Clean Energy, Education and Empowerment Award, the 2012 United Nations Association Global Citizens Award, the 2011 Tech Award, the 2010 Jefferson Award for Public Service, and the 2010 UC Berkeley Chancellor's Award for Civic Engagement.

Laura is on staff at the Blum Center for Developing Economies at the University of California, Berkeley. She has taught in the UC Berkeley School of Public Health and serves on the editorial board for the *Berkeley Wellness Letter*.

**Website:** wecaresolar.org
**Twitter:** @wecaresolar | @lestachel

## CHAPTER 6: LOUISA SILVA

Dr Louisa Silva enjoys practicing medicine in a way that integrates Western medicine, Chinese medicine and Public Health. She had no plans to go into research until the son of a dear friend was diagnosed with autism and she became aware of the devastating lack of options for families. She decided to do something about it. She was awarded grants from Northwest Health Foundation and the Curry Stone Foundation and, over the next ten years, carried out research on a daily parent-delivered massage therapy for autism, based on Chinese medicine. Her research studies have been published. They show that five months of therapy reduces the severity of autism by 25% and improves sleep, digestion and behaviour.

Dr Silva is the first person to show the connection between an abnormal sense of touch and autism, and to research a massage programme whereby parents can normalise their child's sense of touch. She holds a medical degree from UCLA, and a Masters in Public Health and Preventive Medicine from the Medical College of Wisconsin. She lives in Oregon and San Francisco.

**Website:** qsti.org

## CHAPTER 7: LYNN PRICE

Lynn Price is a social entrepreneur, author and inspirational speaker featured on the front page of the US National Speakers Association magazine. With wit, wisdom and compelling stories, she moves corporate and non-profit communities to balance making a living alongside making a difference. Her expertise is Vision For A Change, guiding individuals and groups to bring business ventures to fruition and thrive with the Power of the Ripple to replicate and grow.

Passionate about social responsibility and making change in the world, Lynn is the recipient of the US Points of Light President's Service Award, presented by President Bill Clinton, and Oprah Winfrey's Angel Network Use Your Life Award. Lynn is Founder and President Emeritus of Camp To Belong, an international non-profit organisation dedicated to re-uniting brothers and sisters placed in separate foster homes or other out-of-home care at summer camps and year round experiences. Previously, Lynn was a sales, business development and communications professional with ESPN, Group W Westinghouse Satellite Communications, The Golf Channel and National CineMedia (NCM). She is author of *Vision For A Change: A Social Entrepreneur's Insights from the Heart* and *Real Belonging: Give Siblings Their Right to Reunite* available at amazon.com. Lynn is an Ashoka Fellow, recognised as one of approximately 2,000 global social entrepreneurs around the world.

**Website:** lynnprice.com

## CHAPTER 8: PRITI RADHAKRISHNAN

Priti Radhakrishnan is Co-founder and Director of Treatment Access at I-MAK. She obtained her law degree from New York University (NYU) School of Law and has worked as a health attorney in the United States, Switzerland and India. Prior to founding I-MAK, she served as the Senior Project Officer of the Lawyers Collective HIV/AIDS Unit in India.

In 2007 Priti coordinated the efforts of TEAM VINAY – a movement that registered 25,000 new bone marrow donors in the South Asian American community, which received the National Marrow Donor Program's Lieutenant General Frank E. Peterson Jr. award for innovation and commitment to minority recruitment & retention of bone marrow donors. In 2008, she was awarded the Echoing Green Fellowship for social entrepreneurs, the PopTech Social Innovation Fellowship and was selected as one of 160 dynamic young leaders for the 2008 Asia 21 Young Leaders Summit in Tokyo. The Asia Society also selected Priti as one of three young leaders from the United States for its 2009 Class of Asia 21 Fellows. Priti was awarded the 2010 Black, Latino, Asian Pacific American NYU Law Association's Young Alumni Award. She was named NYU School of Law's Alumnus of the Month (November 2009) and was the 2010 Honoree of the NYU Law Women of Color Collective. Priti was also selected by the King Baudouin Foundation as one of a group of young visionaries making change for its Spotlight on the Millennials series.

In 2011, Priti was named an Associate Fellow by the Asia Society. In 2012 she served as a Mentor at the Unreasonable Institute, an international accelerator for high-impact entrepreneurs. In 2012, Priti was a recipient of the South Asian Bar Association of New York's Legal Trailblazer Award. She is currently serving as a Fellow with the India-Pakistan Regional Young Leaders Forum, as an adjunct faculty member at the St Luke Foundation/Kilimanjaro School of Pharmacy and as Faculty for PopTech's Social Innovation Fellows Program. In 2013, Priti was also awarded the National South Asian Bar Association's Public Interest Achievement Award and was named to the Good 100, a selection of the 100 most innovative individuals changing the world.

**Website:** i-mak.org

# CHAPTER 9: SHARON TERRY

Sharon F. Terry is President and CEO of Genetic Alliance, a network of more than 10,000 organisations, of which 1,200 are disease advocacy organisations. Genetic Alliance enables individuals, families and communities to reclaim their health and become full participants in translational research and services.

She is the founding CEO of PXE International, a research advocacy organisation for the genetic condition pseudoxanthoma elasticum (PXE). As co-discoverer of the gene associated with PXE, she holds the patent for ABCC6 to act as its steward and has assigned her rights to the foundation. She developed a diagnostic test and conducts clinical trials. She is the author of more than 120 peer-reviewed papers, of which 30 are PXE clinical studies.

Sharon is also a co-founder of the Genetic Alliance Registry and Bio-Bank. In her focus at the forefront of consumer participation in genetics research, services and policy, she serves in a leadership role on many of the major international and national organisations, including the Institute of Medicine Science and Policy Board, the IOM Roundtable on Translating Genomic-Based Research for Health, the PubMed Central National Advisory Committee, the National Coalition for Health Professional Education in Genetics Board, the International Rare Disease

Research Consortium Executive Committee and as Founding President of EspeRare Foundation. She is on the editorial boards of several journals. She was instrumental in the passage of the Genetic Information Non-Discrimination Act. In 2005, she received an honorary doctorate from Iona College for her work in community engagement; the first Patient Service Award from the UNC Institute for Pharmacogenomics and Individualized Therapy in 2007; the Research!America Distinguished Organization Advocacy Award in 2009; and, in 2011, the Clinical Research Forum and Foundation's Annual Award for Leadership in Public Advocacy. In 2012, she became an honorary professor of Hebei United University in Tangshan, China, and also received the Facing Our Risk of Cancer Empowered (FORCE) Spirit of Empowerment Advocacy Award. She was named one of FDA's '30 Heroes for the Thirtieth Anniversary of the Orphan Drug Act' in 2013. She is an Ashoka Fellow.

**Website:**  GeneticAlliance.org
**Twitter:**  @sharonfterry | @reg4all | @gabiobank |
@trialsfinder | @babysfirsttest | @genesinlife

## CHAPTER 10: WES JANZ

Wes Janz, PhD, RA, is a professor of architecture at Ball State University, Muncie, Indiana. In 2006, he was the recipient of the university's Outstanding Teaching Award. He is the founder of onesmallproject, a collection of global and local initiatives that foreground the lives of people many observers consider to be in need or at risk. Wes was one of five finalists for the inaugural Curry Stone Design Prize, an international award established in 2008 to recognise and encourage breakthrough projects that 'engage communities at the fulcrum of change, raising awareness, empowering individuals and fostering collective revitalisation.' He is married to Marcia Stone and lives in Indianapolis, Indiana.

**Website:**  onesmallproject.org
**Twitter:**  @onesmallproject

# Further Discussion

1. What do you feel about the use of the word 'reluctant' in this book? Was the editor right not to change it to 'accidental' or 'serendipitous'? Does 'reluctant' innovation lead to more meaningful or lasting solutions?

2. Does everyone have the potential to be a social entrepreneur? Can you learn how to be one, or is it something you are born with?

3. Do you agree that it's better to find your passion, or your calling, before you learn the mechanics of running a social enterprise? What are the advantages of learning first, or getting out in the world first?

4. Is setting out to 'change the world' realistic? Is it even possible? Looking back, how many social entrepreneurs can claim to have done that? Is it realistic to expect to make such a global impact?

5. Why is there a tendency for people to prefer building solutions to the problems of 'others' far away? Why are problems closer to home seen as less attractive? Is there a certain romance to working in Africa or the developing world? What are the pros and cons of such an approach?

6. What common themes run through some, or all, of the stories in this book? How many resonate with you? How many don't? Why?

7.  What are your views on the practicalities – the nuts and bolts – of social innovation after reading this book? Have they changed? Are you surprised by the struggles and challenges many of the innovators in this book faced? Does it put you off?

8.  How can businesses and governments work more closely with social entrepreneurs to shorten the time it takes to research, develop and scale a social innovation?

9.  Do the personal stories of the people behind the innovations matter? Does it help to know what drives them? Does it make social innovation feel 'more real' or achievable?

10. What is the most important attribute of a social entrepreneur? What attributes can you think of?

11. What do you think holds people back from engaging in their innovation, and introducing the vision to others?

12. What are the biggest barriers to innovating solutions to global problems? How might we rectify them?